# HR Burnout

## Reigniting the Flame

By Charli Gamber, SPHR

Evil HR Lady!
All my love,
Charli

Copyright Page



ISBN: 978-0-578-75344-7

This book is presented for informational purposes only. It is not meant to diagnose or treat any illness. If you have a health concern, you should seek the assistance of a medically trained professional.

Before we go any further, let me ask you to stop what you are doing now.

Ease your shoulders, unclench your jaw, and relax your tongue. Take a deep breath. Focus your thoughts on what you are feeling. Allow yourself to experience rest.

Now it is time to address the elephant in the room. Stress is impacting HR at an alarming rate.

Stress is common for everyone today. Caroline Beaton writes, "In all likelihood you know what burnout feels like: exhaustion, disinterest, poor performance, irritability, lack of empathy."[1] It is no secret that our primal fight or flight tendencies no longer serve us in our modern environment. Instead this causes us to react irrationally when we encounter threats that mostly do not require physical responses. There are numerous potential causes of burnout, many of which come into play for HR.

I decided to research burnout because of my own experience working in HR. My peers and I often felt burned out. At first, I heard stories here and there that sounded vaguely similar to mine. Eventually though, there were too many for me to ignore anymore. My own experience drew me to learn more, for my own sake and for others.

I have heard many stories of colleagues and friends who have experienced this during their HR career, and it led me to ask why so many HR professionals are experiencing burnout. Some have chosen to leave HR completely. Some wish to leave but are not sure what else they could do as a career, so they stay and do the best they can. Some just aren't aware that the physical and emotional struggles they are going through are related to what they do for a living. Still, a few have been able to overcome burnout, but those few are rare.

I felt it was important to write this book because of how often I heard stories from talented colleagues going through similar experiences. I also

---

1 When You're Tapped Before Age 30 - https://www.psychologytoday.com/us/blog/the-gen-y-guide/201705/when-youre-tapped-age-30

feeling? Will it ruin your day? Will you let it define you? Or will you take control of your emotions and rise to the occasion? Do you understand how to overcome this?

Does this all sound familiar?

Have these experiences caused you to lose passion for your job or the HR field? Has the quality of your work suffered? Does it make it hard to care about your job, the job that you know is vital to your co-workers, organization, and your own financial and emotional well-being? Have you lost far too much sleep? Do you experience physical symptoms?

For some of you, it may have become so bad that you have tried seeking professional help, taking time off, or upping your self-care game. Others may have looked for new jobs, thinking a new organization would alleviate what they are feeling. Most concerning, some of you have considered looking for a career far removed from HR.

I have spent countless hours wondering what is the root of burnout within HR.

HR professionals are key to the wellness of the organizations we support. We organize wellness initiatives and are asked to recognize the symptoms of burnout in others within the organization. It is a critical role that supports businesses and their employees by developing and reinforcing the culture of the organization.

As professionals, we have done much to improve the way business is done in the majority of organizations. However, we have failed to notice that we are becoming burned out ourselves. Perhaps we have noticed it but are avoiding facing the issue because we are in denial. Individuals may try to push through and get done what needs to be done. Much of that mindset is based in the belief that we are solely responsible for staving off burnout within our organization. If that is true, surely, we can fix our own burnout as well.

When was the last time you felt relaxed? When was the last time you simply stopped moving and did nothing? How long have you felt like this?

# Spark to a Flame

*It's better to burn out, than fade away!*
Def Leppard

As it creeps up on you, you feel your heart racing, your palms become sweaty, uncontrollable tears well up, and you struggle to hold them back. Thoughts race by in a blur and you can't seem to gather them.

"This is not what I need right now," you think. Your tongue feels heavy and you are having trouble forming words. All you can see is red. You may have been feeling off for quite some time. There is a strong possibility you are exhausted or depressed. Maybe you are overly sensitive in comparison to your usual thick-skinned self. You snap at small things that seem disproportionately annoying.

Maybe the experience began with a co-worker's demeaning and rude remarks. Perhaps it was your manager micromanaging you again. It could even be something unrelated to work, such as your son calling you out of the blue with another problem that did not require your attention right that moment or at all. It could have even been your own fault (the most frustrating alternative); you forgot something for an important meeting because you were already overwhelmed and made yourself look foolish. Most of the time, you hold yourself to an impossibly high standard, and sometimes that catches up to you. Often, it is a culmination of events that eventually wears you down, causing you to have a short temper, miss important information, or to become unusually irritable.

When it happens, you excuse yourself and slink into the bathroom or close the door to your office. Once alone, you hang your head in front of you in defeat. Now the question becomes, what are you going to do with this

# Part One:

# Exploring HR Burnout

# Dedication

I dedicate this book to the brave Human Resources professionals who face the challenges of staffing, motivating, and caring for their organizations' people each day. This book would not have happened without the support of Melissa Moerike and Wendy Alexander and my mentor, Nan Poppen. They served as sounding boards and provided feedback to make this book a success. They truly are the epitome of great HR people.

I owe a debt of gratitude to those who participated in the burnout survey as well as those who took additional time to provide feedback regarding their HR burnout experiences or perceptions.

A special thanks to Kate Legters for all the assistance she provided in navigating the data from the survey and the tremendous work she did in editing.

I could not have done this without the support of my friends and family, especially Sara Ehrke, Jessica Mefferd, Kari Kuykendall, Byran Seppanen, and Shawn Birchem.

Last but not least, I dedicate this book to Mr. Peanut, because he is always there for me.

# Contents


- Dedication 4
- Exploring HR Burnout 5
  - Spark to a Flame 6
  - HR Career Paths 13
  - The Passing of the Torch - On History 21
  - Causes 32
    - Heat: Personality/Demographics 33
    - Oxygen: Environment 43
    - Fuel: Stress/Critical Events 50
  - Withdrawal – The End 65
- Solutions 70
  - Time Management 71
  - Career Management 83
  - Stress Management 91
  - Global Solutions 103
- Appendix 110
  - HR Burnout Survey Results 110
  - Maslach Burnout Inventory 122

had experienced my own burnout. My hope is that in exploring HR burnout and learning all we can about it, we will help to ward off burnout within the profession and beyond.

I distinctly recall the first time that I faced burnout. I had been recently laid off from an HR position and was sitting in a meeting surrounded by other HR professionals. Looking around the room, I remember I did not feel a particular connection with these colleagues. I thought in horror, "What does this mean about me? What does it mean for the work that I do?" I began to wonder if I'd chosen the right career path.

I thought perhaps it meant that what I do is not valued by the world. Also, it was extremely concerning as I did not know what I would do if I was not in HR. There is nothing else that I feel called to do and I wondered if I was qualified to do anything else. HR had been my identity for over a decade, but now I felt disconnected, inadequate, afraid, and uncertain. The isolation and uncertainty almost certainly made what I was feeling more difficult to go through.

After this experience, I began to hear from other HR professionals who felt similarly or had gone through similar experiences and were not sure that they wanted to stay in HR. At some point it all clicked. There seemed to be a pattern. The universe was shouting at me, forcing me to look in this direction. As I started to research burnout, it saddened me how common the experience was amongst HR professionals. Eventually, I surrendered to its demanding voice and started to learn about the phenomenon our profession is facing. What exactly is burnout though?

Definitions vary. Jeanine Joy writes, "[b]urnout is the result of chronic stress, largely from one's work, when an individual has inadequate stress management and coping skills for the stress they're experiencing. This definition explains why two people in equivalent circumstances can have different outcomes."[2] The Mayo Clinic defines burnout as, "a type of job stress in which you might feel physically, mentally, and emotionally

---

2 https://www.quora.com/What-professions-do-you-feel-have-the-highest-incidences-of-burnout-and-why

exhausted. You might also question your career choice and the value of your contribution at work."[3] Described as a type of stress, office burnout can manifest itself as a state of physical, emotional, or mental exhaustion combined with doubts about your competence and the value of your work itself.[4] Cristina Maslach, one of the first researchers of burnout and an expert in the field, defines burnout as "...a state of exhaustion in which one is cynical about the value of one's occupation and doubtful of one's capacity to perform."[5] Essentially, burnout is what happens when you are exposed to work stress for too long and your coping mechanisms can no longer hold it off. Burnout is your reaction to prolonged and unmitigated stress. One of the ongoing challenges with burnout is that it has not been defined and researched thoroughly, and it leaves much room for interpretation.[6] There is definitely a need for more research and clarification to burnout. This is one of the limitations and may cause some of our own confusion in recognizing the condition. It is a deeply personal experience and is different for each individual who experiences it. Your body and/or mind may simply give up if burnout is allowed to continue for too long.

My career progression is one that is not that uncommon in the HR world. I had an inspirational experience with an Office Manager named Susan during one of my first jobs while in high school. She opened my eyes to how much human resources could change work and life for employees. Initially when planning for college, I had considered a career in education, which led me to Southwest Minnesota State University (SMSU) in Marshall, MN. By the time I enrolled in classes, I had decided to pursue HR instead. I was heavily involved in SMSU's SHRM (Society for Human Resource Management) chapter during my four years there. I spent my last two years of school as an HR/safety intern, learning the basics of HR.

---

3 https://stress.lovetoknow.com/Which_Professionals_are_Prone_to_Burnout

4 https://www.growthbusiness.co.uk/jobs-likely-cause-burn-out-2550536/

5 https://www.wilmarschaufeli.nl/publications/Schaufeli/311.pdf

6 https://journals.sagepub.com/doi/full/10.1177/2158244017697154

After school, I worked a factory job before I landed my first "real" job in HR. That was in 2009, a tough time to find a job in HR, even with two years of internship experience under my belt. However, I was fortunate. Menards was seeking an HR Coordinator to join their team and required a Bachelor's degree in HR for the job at that time.

I worked for the next ten years in increasingly challenging HR roles. Some of my experience was with organizations that had some degree of corporate HR support. However, some of my time in HR, I consisted of a department of one. This can be lonely and you have to be able to bootstrap yourself.

Simultaneously, I continued volunteering in HR. I have served extensively as a SHRM volunteer and I founded the Sioux Falls chapter of DisruptHR. I am a firm believer in connecting, mentoring, and learning with HR peers. In March of 2017, I was laid off from my role. Once again, I was fortunate. I saw the layoff coming and planned ahead. At the time, I was finishing up my Master's of Science in HR from Southern New Hampshire University.

The job market in HR in Sioux Falls was competitive and jobs were scarce. In order to find a new role in line with my career path, I relocated. That gave me a lot of time to reflect on what was important to me, where my career had led, and where it would continue to take me.

I found myself thinking for the first time about whether HR was the right career for me. Since my undergraduate degree, HR had always been a clear choice for me, but now for the first time I doubted my chosen career path. In over ten years in HR, I had been privileged to do incredible things. I had meaningful and life-changing interactions with employees and had developed deep and committed relationships with colleagues, co-workers, and managers.

On the flip side, I also had employees lose their patience with me for things that were out of my control. I have had to be the bearer of bad news to employees and managers, and many have not taken it well. I have laid employees off and been the one to look an employee in the eye and tell them that their livelihood was being stripped from them, a harrowing experience. Those conversations were difficult whether the cause was due to their actions or not. There were also times I fought for employees to be taken care of and was able to make a positive impact on the employee's life.

After ten years, I found myself questioning if this was what I wanted to do for the rest of my life.

Disclosing this has been insightful for me and has also helped me reflect on what I have struggled with, what my particular challenges have been, and what has been most helpful for my path moving forward. There is a fear that goes along with opening up, about letting others see what I have been through. Individuals will read this and draw their own conclusions. Some may agree with me; some will not. Ultimately, the price of disclosing my experience and the research I have done is worth it if it helps others whose experiences are similar.

&&

# HR Career Paths

*She's living in a world and it's on fire.*
Alicia Keys

HR tends to function in the middle of the organization in several ways. It reminds me of professor Dr. Gochenouer saying during my business capstone that HR was doing their job properly when everyone hated them. What I have come to learn is that it is not far from the truth.

HR serves as employee advocate and business partner. Those two things often intersect but not always. We may be called to deliver bad news to employees. We may tell them they are being fired, their paycheck will not be on time, their benefits are not set up as they expected, and so on.

We also deliver negative news to managers. There are times we have to inform them they cannot fire an employee because they have not adequately documented the situation. That news is a perennial sticking point. Inevitably, in order to serve the business best, our goal is to keep the needs of all stakeholders in mind and balance the competing priorities carefully. It is not an easy position to be in and the decisions we make are often challenging ones.

We know that individuals find themselves in HR in many different ways. Some stumble into HR from office management or related fields. SHRM research shows, "[p]rior to becoming a generalist, about half of those we interviewed held other HR positions or jobs that overlapped with HR."[7] That means about half of us come from HR, or a related field, and half of us come from other fields. Some pursue a degree in HR first. Some come to

7 www.shrmorg/hr-today/trends-and-forecasting/research-and-surveys/pages/hr-careers-research-2017-interviews.aspx

the field with degrees in psychology, law, or other areas. Many choose the field because they want to "help others." To be honest, some choose careers in HR because they believe it will be an easy desk job where they will have access to everyone else's business. We all have different motivations for pursuing our career in HR. SHRM also found that not quite half of us "fell" into HR.[8] The field has an almost infinitely diverse number of members in it.

Many start in an entry level role. Maybe they are an HR Assistant or a Payroll Clerk. They file. In fact, we often want two years of experience in order for them to file. SHRM found that "[m]any entry-level HR positions advertised in the paper or online require one or more years' experience, and it is for this reason that SHRM emphasizes the importance of taking advantage of HR internships while still in school—or immediately after graduating."[9] This experience is frequently gained through internships, temporary roles, a job as a recruiter at a staffing company, or in a related field that allows the incumbent to transfer into the role.

Some start higher up in the organization or eventually are promoted. According to an article by SHRM, "Others may start out at small organizations without an HR department. As the organization grows, they will eventually need to establish an HR department and an opportunity may arise."[10] Some stay with one organization for over twenty years, while some move up the ranks in different organizations. Perhaps, they are satisfied with the level that they start in or perhaps they work themselves up the corporate ladder. Some handle accounting and office management and wear HR as another one of their hats. Those that work their way up may become an HR Manager, or an HR Director, or a VP of HR. Perhaps they make their way to CHRO (Chief Human Resources Officer). Some of us

---

8 www.shrmorg/hr-today/trends-and-forecasting/research-and-surveys/pages/hr-careers-research-2017-interviews.aspx

9 www.shrm.org/membership/student-resources-pages/careersinhrm.aspx

10 www.shrm.org/membership/student-resources-pages/careersinhrm.aspx

are laid off. Some of us get fired. These things can happen in all different careers, too.

The positions are as varied as the career path, and we work in publicly traded and privately held companies, profit and non-profit sectors, private industry and government agencies, as generalists or specialists, and in departments of one or specializing as a function in a department of hundreds or thousands. Regardless of what your HR position looks like, there is a certain amount of pride that goes into having selected HR as a career. HR is a good career. "In fact, in 2007, *Money* magazine and Salary.com researched hundreds of jobs and ranked Human Resource Manager as number four on its list of the Top Ten Best Jobs in America based on a variety of factors, including job growth in the next decade, earnings potential, creativity and flexibility."[11] How then do you go from pride and excitement about your career choice to experiencing HR burnout?

The concepts here could be applied outside the HR profession, but that is not my intent with this book. What is crucial here: helping our profession, a profession that often dedicates itself to helping other professions. Sure, expanding your awareness about the causes, symptoms, and cures of burnout will help you support others who experience burnout in the future. This is a "put your own oxygen mask on first" concept. If you are not in proper working condition, how could you possibly be able to help others? We must become more self-aware in order to survive to support others another day. **We have to become ruthlessly selfish in pursuit of our own well-being.** We have to put the needs of others aside and focus inward. We have to be willing to put ourselves first for once.

The world and our little section of it are changing at a rapid pace. We are engaged in the "War for Talent," we are being called on more than ever before to solve the biggest problems in our organizations, and we are claiming our seat at the table and providing our viewpoints on strategy. Throughout the changes of the last few years, many of us have worked

---

11 www.shrm.org/membership/student-resources-pages/careersinhrm.aspx

valiantly to get our field and our organizations to this point. Unfortunately, some of us have reached the point of exhaustion. Very little research has been conducted on burnout in HR professionals. SHRM, the largest professional society dedicated to HR professionals has an approximately 3000 word article on this.[12] Nothing else can be found in the SHRM store when you search for burnout, even while the articles on burnout in HR are rapidly coming forward.

Why is that? Why does a profession that is dedicated to monitoring the safety and wellbeing of its employees ignore its own burnout? Is it because we are supposed to look out for others in this area, to serve as an expert in this, so surely, we cannot experience it ourselves? Is it because HR is a fairly recently developed professional career? Is it because of the changes occurring rapidly within our field? Have we just been too busy to notice? As I started thinking about this topic, there were so many questions and so few answers. I had to go find the answers. I felt compelled.

In preparation for this book, I conducted a survey of HR professionals to gather their experiences on burnout. Once the survey results were collected, I interviewed willing respondents and reviewed other sources to get a complete picture about what HR burnout looks like and best practices in avoiding and overcoming burnout. I believe this topic is so important that I dedicated myself to this research and to helping my fellow HR colleagues who have experienced or may be at risk for experiencing burnout.

I published the survey late one Sunday evening. I woke up to a handful of responses the next morning, which I had not expected. After work, I checked again, and there were 28 responses. The responses continued to pour in. I was concerned that the responses would be those who were particularly passionate about burnout as they were experiencing it, but the responses ranged from deeply concerned about HR burnout to not concerned at all. Some of us seem to be fairing pretty well. What was allowing them to skate through unscathed by burnout? As much as the

---

12 https://www.shrm.org/hr-today/news/hr-magazine/pages/0703covstory.aspx

concerning responses caught my attention, I wanted to dig into the ones who were thriving in particular.

There were a number of dire responses. Burnout in our field is not uncommon. Initially, I was not able to ascertain any commonalities in the data. As the responses came in, I became increasingly horrified, concerned, and frankly, a little angry. Our people are hurting. The results of the survey are published as an appendix to this book for your review and the answers are incorporated throughout the book.

Burnout is not solely an HR problem. We as HR professionals recognize that. "The biggest threat to building an engaged workforce in 2017 is employee burnout. The newest study in the Employee Engagement Series conducted by Kronos Incorporated and Future Workplace® found 95 percent of human resource leaders admit employee burnout is sabotaging workforce retention, yet there is no obvious solution on the horizon."[13] How common is burnout in the overall population? "Some studies report burnout prevalence rates of up to 69% in a given population...more cautious and conservative studies estimate the prevalence of burnout to be above 10%."[14] Estimates vary depending on the method used to collect it and who you ask, but there is no doubt that it is a serious issue deserving of attention.

Other professions experience burnout challenges, too. The medical profession is often recognized as having the highest levels of burnout. Dr. Jeanine Joy writes, "[m]ore than half of the physicians in the United States have at least one symptom of burnout."[15] "The American Medical Association estimates that almost 50% of physicians experience symptoms of serious job burnout, attributed in part due to the demands and stress of patient care, long hours, and increasing administrative burdens."[16] In a

---

13 https://www.kronos.com/about-us/newsroom/employee-burnout-crisis-study-reveals-big-workplace-challenge-2017

14 https://journals.sagepub.com/doi/full/10.1177/2158244017697154

15 https://www.quora.com/What-professions-do-you-feel-have-the-highest-incidences-of-burnout-and-why

16 https://stress.lovetoknow.com/Which_Professionals_are_Prone_to_Burnout

2013 study of senior management, 50% believed their CEO was burned out and 75% believed their fellow senior managers were burned out.[17] Nursing, social workers, teachers, principals, attorneys, police officers, accountants, fast food and retail workers are all considered particularly at risk for burnout as well.[18] Now, take a look at the reasons attributed to these professions:

| Profession | Reason for High Burnout |
|---|---|
| Nursing | High nurse-to-patient ratios, long shifts |
| Social workers | Working with clients spills over into their personal lives |
| Principal | Ongoing and constant pressures of their jobs |
| Attorney | Nature of working in a field that focuses on problems |
| Police officer | High stress situations, exposed to the worst of human nature on an ongoing basis |
| Accounting | Frequent busy travel, crazy tax season, quarterly filing deadlines |
| Fast food | Low pay, monotonous tasks |
| Retail | Environment where employees do not feel valued by management[19] |

Notice any similarities? I am not saying that our jobs are as stressful as police officers, but it is easy to read through this list and see similarities to what we do in HR. Helping fields also seem to be particularly susceptible to overwhelming stress. These fields also tend to face higher burnout rates than average. It would be hard to deny that one's field of choice impacts the likelihood that one experiences burnout.

Resilience is another potential factor. The Global Resilience Report 2018 created by the Resilience Institute found that those working in insurance, pharmaceuticals, government, energy, and professional services have more

---

17 https://www.tlnt.com/c-level-burnout-a-problem-no-one-talks-about/

18 https://stress.lovetoknow.com/Which_Professionals_are_Prone_to_Burnout

19 https://stress.lovetoknow.com/Which_Professionals_are_Prone_to_Burnout

resilience than those in food and beverages, education, finance, human services, and construction.[20] Resilience is widely regarded as a mitigating factor to burnout; if you have resilience, you are less likely to experience burnout. What is it about those in these fields that make them more resilient? And how can we as HR professionals harness that and use it for our own good?

These lists consistently leave out HR though. Dawn Burke's anecdotal experience through her speaking engagements indicates approximately 75% of HR professionals indicate they are experiencing burnout.[21] My research found that burnout occurs in HR professionals at an alarming rate; 55.9% of respondents indicated they had experienced HR burnout and another 13.6% said they felt they were on the verge. Regardless of the exact percentages, burnout is an incredible problem that organizations face today. Dr. Jeanine Joy writes, "[i]n 2015, for all industries, the global burden of burnout cost is in excess of $300 billion annually."[22] According to Charlie DeWitt, Vice President of Business Development at Kronos, "[e]mployee burnout has reached epidemic proportions."[23] I would argue that HR burnout is reaching epidemic proportions itself.

Of interest, "Cherniss and Kranz (1983) discovered that there was relatively no burnout in Montessori schools, monasteries, and religious care centers. Others equated the lack of burnout in these organizations to shared values, social commitment, and a sense of communion."[24] This is fascinating. Of course, we need to understand how they are managing to not experience any burnout when the rest of us are experiencing so much burnout. Given

---

20 https://2krnrx3k2ieq4dsbl743vvpn-wpengine.netdna-ssl.com/wp-content/uploads/2018/08/Resilience-Enables-Strategic-Agility-2018.pdf

21 http://fistfuloftalent.com/2018/11/4-indicators-ceo-interested-in-burnout.html

22 https://www.quora.com/What-professions-do-you-feel-have-the-highest-incidences-of-burnout-and-why

23 https://www.kronos.com/about-us/newsroom/employee-burnout-crisis-study-reveals-big-workplace-challenge-2017

24 scholarworks.umt.edu/cgi/viewcontent.cgi?article=1454&context=etd

that, I would like to think there is hope for us, hope that we can use what we can learn here to overcome our burnout.

My message in this book is that we must take responsibility and accountability for our own lives, and as much as we possibly can in our circumstances, for our own organizations. If we are not happy with where we are at, we have to be the ones to change that. Only we have the power to make those decisions. If we are unhappy, it is our own damn fault. I am not saying that you control everything. I am not saying that you deserve people being jerks to you, or being stuck in a dead-end job, or needing to have a paycheck and feeling like you have to make this job work because of that simple fact. I am saying that if you do not like it, you are the only one who will be able to change it. We do not control everything, but there are many important things that are under your control. Without that belief, you may end up hopeless.

The world is full of stories of people who have overcome unbearably difficult things in order to be happy. It brings to mind Viktor Frankl's epic work, *Man's Search for Meaning*. Frankl survived the Holocaust and went on to write his story, which is harrowing. It is hard to imagine an experience more desperate than being held in a concentration camp. Even in a situation where we get to control nothing, we always get the right to choose our reaction and in our reaction lies our destiny.

## The Passing of the Torch - On History

*We didn't start the fire; it was always burning since the world's been turning.*
Billy Joel

Burnout is not a new phenomenon. The earliest reference to burnout was quite possibly the "weariness of Elijah." [25] There are occasional references to it in other literary works as well. "Rösing describes 'burnout' among the Quechua and Aymarai Indians from the Andes...and among the Ladakhs in the Himalaya...calling it a 'loss of soul', in which exhaustion plays an important role, together with feelings of meaninglessness and emptiness."[26] In 1869, American neurologist George Miller Beard named a new disease "neurasthenia," which he described as reduced energy due to a faster pace of life. The disease was characterized by mental and physical exhaustion. Neurasthenia was a common diagnosis for businessmen of the day. [27] While it does appear that burnout could be traced back to ancient times, it is much more commonly reported today.

Amongst the social revolution of the 1960s, the expertise of many of the helping professions was eroded. Now, they were expected to work harder for the respect they were so freely given previously. The recipients of their care expected higher levels of care and consideration. "From the perspective of social exchange, a discrepancy grew between the professionals' efforts and the rewards they received in terms of recognition

25 https://www.ncbi.nlm.nih.gov/pmc/articles/PMC3230825/

26 https://www.wilmarschaufeli.nl/publications/Schaufeli/481.pdf

27 https://www.wilmarschaufeli.nl/publications/Schaufeli/481.pdf

and gratitude. This 'lack of reciprocity' is known to foster burnout."[28] Bäuerle D. "describes the classical burnout victims of the 1970s and 1980s as people who failed to reach unrealistically high altruistic goals, people who, at least on the surface, had been idealists."[29] The demands of modern professions continue to rise.

These demands have started to take their toll. In the 1970s, the Japanese coined the word "karoshi" which means to literally work one's self to death.[30] Employees were working so much that they were passing away due to various causes, sometimes right at their desks at work. Japanese employees wear this as a badge of honor. The time spent at the employer is viewed as a valuable investment in the company and if they move on to another company, they have to start over from scratch and reinvest all those wasted hours. This is one example, albeit an extreme one, of burnout's potential impact.

The term "burnout" was coined in 1974 in the United States by Herbert Freudenberger. He noted a close relationship between burnout and depression, identifying the difference as burnout was "job related and situation specific rather than general and pervasive" as in depression.[31] Sigmund Ginsburg also published an article that year referencing burnout; however, Freudenberger's pursuit of the term means that he is often viewed as the "founding-father of the concept."[32] At this same time, Maslach was discovering burnout was common amongst human services workers. The symptoms she found included "emotional exhaust[ion]...negative perceptions and feelings about their clients...and that they experienced crises in professional competence as a result of this emotional turmoil."[33] Maslach is the creator of the Maslach Burnout

---

28 https://www.wilmarschaufeli.nl/publications/Schaufeli/481.pdf

29 https://www.ncbi.nlm.nih.gov/pmc/articles/PMC3230825/

30 https://www.businessinsider.com/what-is-karoshi-japanese-word-for-death-by-overwork-2017-10

31 https://www.ncbi.nlm.nih.gov/pmc/articles/PMC3230825/

32 https://journals.sagepub.com/doi/full/10.1177/2158244017697154

33 https://www.wilmarschaufeli.nl/publications/Schaufeli/481.pdf

Inventory (MBI), which is the most commonly used indicator of burnout.[34] The MBI was revolutionary because it meant we had a way to quantify burnout and compare it between professions. It is interesting that during this timeframe, burnout was simultaneously receiving so much attention from different parties for the first time in history. The 1970s generated burnout's mainstream acceptance.

As Maslach continued her work, burnout was mainly considered to be a human services disease. "Tellingly, burnout discussions began within the human services, because they were better able to give 'voice' to issues of emotions, values, and relationships with people..."[35] Burnout is often seen in the helping professions and professions where processing others' emotions is common. Burnout was viewed as a natural response to turning the "helping professions from callings into modern occupations."[36] Here was a group of professionals, deeply dedicated to the work they had hand selected and experiencing the frustration of not being able to achieve their ideals. Over time, the expectations were raised and the resources and rewards were (at least in their eyes) lowered. "The experience of burnout was not merely an inconvenience or an occupational hazard, but a devastating attack on their professional identity."[37] Merely being tired could not adequately define their disappointment. Furthermore, the theory exists that the organizational values and the personal values of these human services professionals in part caused their burnout.[38] The disconnect between the employees' beliefs and the organization's beliefs primed them for burnout.

Eventually, it became clear that burnout was not strictly related to human services and could be experienced in other professions and trades. It does seem to have historically impacted those whose careers are intended to

---

34 https://www.quora.com/What-professions-do-you-feel-have-the-highest-incidences-of-burnout-and-why

35 https://www.wilmarschaufeli.nl/publications/Schaufeli/311.pdf

36 https://www.wilmarschaufeli.nl/publications/Schaufeli/481.pdf

37 https://www.wilmarschaufeli.nl/publications/Schaufeli/311.pdf

38 https://www.wilmarschaufeli.nl/publications/Schaufeli/481.pdf

help others more and earlier. Today, burnout is seen as very common in North America, possibly because it is not considered a medical diagnosis there and carries fewer consequences; it is viewed as the opposite in some European countries, opening up individuals suffering from burnout to potential resources such as medical treatment or disability benefits but also to the stigma attached with mental health diagnoses.[39] Still today, there is "neither an officially accepted definition nor a valid instrument for the differential diagnosis of burnout syndrome."[40] This obviously leads to challenges with defining and diagnosing burnout, along with treatment and prevention.

The amount of research put into burnout is staggering and continues to grow. Burnout is generally viewed as causing "emotional exhaustion, depersonalization, and reduced performance ability and/or motivation."[41] It has generated much discussion and research into "emotional labor, symptom contagion, and social exchange."[42] In other words, burnout is creating personal, organizational, and societal concerns that are impacting more than the individual experiencing burnout. The lack of recognition of burnout as a medical diagnosis in the United States creates problems for those experiencing it here. While one could pursue a diagnosis of depression and pursue benefits including time off, treatment, disability, or other benefits by going that route, depression and burnout are not quite the same thing. While they share many similarities, depression does not have quite the same work-related connotations that burnout does.

When you look across the history of burnout and what was happening in the affected fields, it is easy to draw conclusions about what has happened in the HR field resulting in our mass burnout. Think about how burnout developed amongst the human services professionals during the 1970s and compare that to how burnout has been experienced by modern HR professionals. These individuals went into their chosen profession to help

---

39 https://www.wilmarschaufeli.nl/publications/Schaufeli/481.pdf

40 https://www.ncbi.nlm.nih.gov/pmc/articles/PMC3230825/

41 https://www.ncbi.nlm.nih.gov/pmc/articles/PMC3230825/

42 https://www.wilmarschaufeli.nl/publications/Schaufeli/311.pdf

others and create change. They experienced burnout when they were not able to achieve these goals. They had also experienced increased demands and fewer resources to achieve these demands. Their very identities were threatened by the circumstances. Finally, organizational values and personal values were not in alignment. Think of the parallels between their circumstances and ours as HR professionals. Personally, I can see my own experiences here and have heard of other HR professionals who have had similar experiences.

I have outlined the history of the HR field to guide in understanding the role that burnout has played. Human resources has its roots in the Industrial Revolution (1760-1840) and is widely believed to be the brainchild of Robert Owen. In fact, Robert Owen is known as the Father of Personnel Management.[43] He believed that improving the worker's situation, often dreary in these times, would result in a return for the organization. Prior to this time frame, all positions were intrinsically defined by what the employee did, i.e. butcher, blacksmith, seamstress. The Industrial Revolution led to more work being performed by a specialist within an organization rather than as one lone individual, which in turn caused a decrease in the individual's control over their work as we shifted from self-employment to employment for others. For example, hours worked increased, working conditions worsened, and most employees had little to no say in how work was performed. At this time, most business owners did not recognize the value that improving working conditions would have on worker productivity or it was considered an afterthought at most.[44] Robert Owen was one of the first pioneers of shortening the work day to allow employees an opportunity to rest. "He proved that commercial success could be achieved without exploitation of those employed; his approach to social and economic organisation [sic] was extended beyond the mill floor to every aspect of village life."[45] A very forward-thinking approach, indeed!

---

43 www.whatishumanresource.com/robert-owen

44 https://www.turbinehq.com/blog/history-of-hr

45 www.whatishumanresource.com/robert-owen

Despite this early foray into HR, most would not recognize the importance of care for the organization's employees until later on. Workers had no collective bargaining rights and no one served as employee advocate in most organizations at this time. Frederick Taylor wrote his book *Shop Management* in 1900 recommending training, incentives, and performance management of employees to improve business objectives.[46] The first Personnel department was established by the National Cash Register Company in 1901 after a strike. Their primary responsibilities included safety, wages, recordkeeping, and resolving employee grievances.[47] This was the first of many departments established within organizations to resolve employee issues, setting the stage for the modern HR department. In fact, in 1913, the Welfare Workers' Association, the first human resources association, was created in England. It would later become the Chartered Institute of Personnel and Development, after several name changes.[48] "Personnel administration, which emerged as a clearly defined field by the 1920s (at least in the US), was largely concerned with the technical aspects of hiring, evaluating, training, and compensating employees..."[49] The original HR department was born and had begun organizing and networking.

In the 1920s, Elton Mayo conducted the Hawthorne studies at the Western Electric Company to better understand worker behavior.[50] These studies were initially looking at unrelated items such as how improving lighting would result in productivity increases. What they actually found was the presence of the researchers itself had a more pronounced effect on worker productivity, today referred to as the Hawthorne effect. Basically, when a person is observed, he or she will change his or her behavior. This revelation provided an additional springboard for employment reform and

---

46 www.whatishumanresource.com/robert/owen

47 www.fastcompany.com/3045829/welcome-to-the-new-era-of-human-resources

48 https://en.wikipedia.org/wiki/Chartered_Institute_of_Personnel_and_Development

49 http://www.whatishumanresource.com/the-historical-background-of-human-resource-management

50 https://courses.lumenlearning.com/wmopen-introbusiness/chapter/the-hawthorne-studies/

change, modernizing our understanding of human behavior and guiding future human resources professionals.

The National Labor Relations Act (also known as the Wagner Act) was passed in 1935, creating the National Labor Relations Board and allowing employees to create unions and bargain collectively.[51] This could be considered the point where the pendulum begins to swing in employees' favor, leading to a need for more developed HR functions to manage the changing employment landscape and the increasing demands placed on organizations. "[T]he near-simultaneous rise of trade unions and personnel management departments within companies laid the groundwork for the formal discipline of human resources."[52] Union membership was widespread from 1945-1965. Organizations needed HR departments to manage the growing complications of complying with the laws and managing the relationship between management and the labor force.

In 1945, Cornell University in New York responded by establishing the "School of Industrial and Labour Relations," the first official HR program.[53] The American Society for Personnel Administration (ASPA) formed in 1948. It would eventually become the Society for Human Resource Management (SHRM), the largest organization dedicated to serving the HR function worldwide.[54] Union membership peaked shortly after in 1954.[55] The need for HR departments was cemented.

Possibly the most impactful document on the state of HR since its inception, Title VII of the Civil Rights Act of 1964, again affirmed the need for HR departments. Around this same time, affirmative action was created by Executive Orders.[56] The Civil Rights Act made way for the Civil Rights Movement. Legislation protecting workers' rights continues to be passed,

---

51 www.nlrb.gov/who-we-are/our-history/1935-passage-wagner-act

52 www.humanresourcesmba.net/faq/what-is-the-history-of-human-resources/

53 https://www.ilr.cornell.edu/about-ilr

54 www.willamette.edu/org/shrm/about/index.html

55 http://www.pewresearch.org/fact-tank/2014/02/20/for-american-unions-membership-trails-far-behind-public-support/

56 https://www.hg.org/legal-articles/what-is-affirmative-action-and-why-was-it-created-31524

affording employees additional rights. By the 1980s "human resource management" as a term had gained common acceptance.[57] Employees and management were learning what their HR departments were there for and began to rely on them heavily as an answer to any employee issue. "HRM developed in response to the substantial increase in competitive pressures American business organizations began experiencing by the late 1970s as a result of such factors as globalization, deregulation, and rapid technological change."[58] Modern changes have increased the demands on HR and continue to change HR's role in the organization. HR continues to develop from their original use as an administrative and compliance role to one of partnering with the business to strategically direct the organization's human capital.

This covering of the history of HR is intended to show where the profession has come from and how modern HR has sprung from a compliance/administrative role to one of strategic importance within the business. HR has clearly become more complicated as the business world has become increasingly diversified, globalized, and technological. From humble beginnings, the HR profession has changed the relationship between employees and employers. "The history of human resources is a rich and complex one, shaped by fields including business and psychology as well as the civil rights movement and legal cases dealing with workers' rights." [59] These changes are far from over. Each day brings new challenges, new legislation, and new perspectives.

What conclusions can be drawn from comparing the history of burnout and the history of HR? Burnout has existed for some period of time and appears to be possible across different cultures, although it is experienced differently within different cultures. Historical data is limited but burnout appears to be increasing across many professions. The growing interest in

---

57 https://www.turbinehq.com/blog/history-of-hr

58 http://www.academia.edu/6464898/THE_DEVELOPMENT_OF_HUMAN_RESOURCE_MANAGEMENT_FROM_A_HISTORICAL_PERSPECTIVE_AND_ITS_ IMPLICATIONS_FOR_THE_HUMAN_RESOURCE_MANAGER

59 www.humanresourcesmba.net/faq/what-is-the-history-of-human-resources/

the topic can be used as anecdotal evidence that the problem has gotten worse over time. This may be related to changes in our society such as increased speed at which we encounter change and information, and constant connectivity making us always feel "on." Hours have steadily increased since the Industrial Revolution, too.

HR is a fairly recently developed profession. It continues to develop and we continue to improve our techniques. There is always room for improved analytics and understanding of the employees and organizations we represent. Each of us experiences our own growth and journeys throughout our careers. Given how new HR is, we will most likely continue to experience additional change, again hopefully for the better. Imagine the difference between the first established HR department and the first time HR was given a "seat at the table." Now imagine how much additional change could take place in the next hundred years. Think about how much change happened in your career to date so far and what could happen before you retire.

HR tends to be a field where much is expected and little is received in return. It can be a thankless job. Lack of reciprocity is common. We represent employees and management and are often stuck between the two as mediator. Often, we offer a solution that does not completely satisfy either party in that circumstance. Upon resolution, HR professionals feel no one is satisfied despite giving their best efforts each day. As Dr. Nadine Greiner eloquently put it, "Nobody cares about HR. People rarely understand what we do."[60] It can be very lonely working in HR. The experience is not unlike that of human service professionals and our trajectory of burnout is likely to continue to follow theirs. Many HR professionals also feel called to the profession. This could indicate that they may experience some of the idealism that human services professionals experienced that may have encouraged their burnout.

HR is a function that in most organizations is relegated to the side lines, and not viewed as a main player in the game. We are viewed as a "support"

---

60 Personal interview with Dr. Nadine Greiner, November 19, 2018.

function. Our worth is determined by how much "support" we provide. If the labor market is tight and we cannot hire enough employees, we are to blame. We failed to overcome the external forces affecting our organizations. If we are tasked with reinforcing compliance and government regulations are particularly stringent, we are often blamed, even if we are only the messenger. Furthermore, HR is brought in retroactively when something is identified as wrong with an employee and a manager wants it addressed; generally, HR is not included as a partner who is proactively approached to solve business problems. Often HR is brought in to resolve the problems that a manager has procrastinated on, such as managing a problem employee. While this is an overly cynical view, it is also not an uncommon description of many HR professionals' experiences within their organization.

Additionally, we often feel like we are working against managers or employees who do not understand what we do. It is our responsibility to educate our team on what we do. However, we know that sometimes this falls on deaf ears. HR is rarely allowed to be selfish, to ensure that our needs are met. Our work creates outcomes for others, and HR often works selflessly for the goals of the business and individual employees. We take this burden on ourselves typically. We are relied on to advocate for employees, leaving us responsible for the emotional work of other parties, which can be exhausting and fruitless work. Our work is deeply relationship-oriented, which can be both rewarding and challenging. Personally, I have found the most challenging work to also be some of the most rewarding when the breakthrough is achieved. This does not mean that the challenges do not take their toll as they are experienced.

We have also seen our profession become increasingly complex and the standards have been raised considerably. An HR professional must be an expert in all of the many areas of HR, be a strategic partner, have a seat at the table, and have business acumen. Technology, psychology, and global circumstances evolve constantly. As we achieve more, the expectations also increase, allowing us to become more susceptible to burnout.

In 2019, the World Health Organization included burnout in its International Classification of Diseases. It is still not listed in the DSM-5, the United States' reference for diseases.[61] The history of burnout continues to evolve from year to year and acceptance of burnout as a serious concern is increasingly common. Like all things, it takes time. The history of HR and the history of burnout have had their own trajectories, with some insightful overlap occurring.

61 https://abcnews.go.com/GMA/Wellness/burnout-now-official-medical-diagnosis/story?id=63316174

ở৵ᡐ

# Causes

*We were strikin' the matches, right down to the ashes, setting the world on fire.*

Kenny Chesney/Pink

Perhaps the cause of burnout is encapsulated in its title...burnout. As an analogy, turn to the similarities between burnout and fire. The three elements of a fire are illustrated below: oxygen, heat, and fuel. In the burnout version, heat is personality/demographic factors, oxygen is environmental factors, and the fuel is stress or critical events. To create burnout, I believe all three of these factors must be present and in satisfying quantities, as their corresponding components have to be for a physical fire to start. This chapter will explain how these three factors contribute individually to burnout and culminate in burnout. Each of these elements can make you more inclined to burnout or can have a mitigating effect on your burnout, depending on how they manifest.

I would argue that in order for burnout to occur, you have to have a personality that is susceptible to burnout. If this condition is met, then you have to be in an environment that will lead to burnout. Finally, once these conditions are met, stressful events occur that cause burnout. The three components build on one another and are interrelated.

**Figure 1: Framework for Burnout**

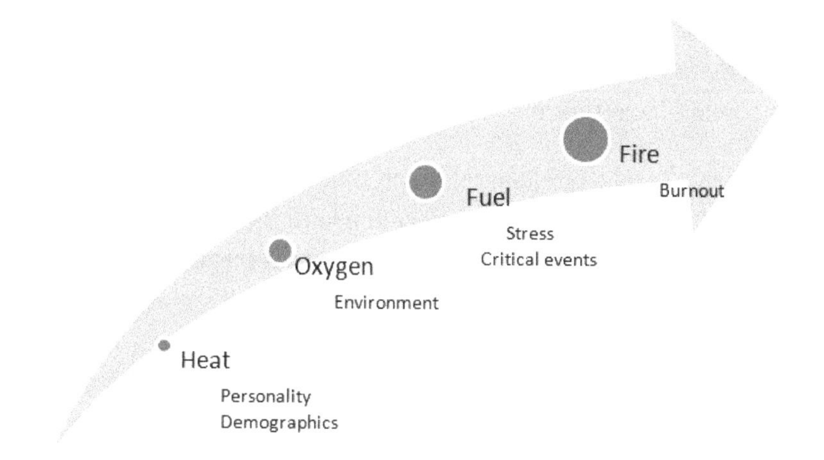


# Heat: Personality/Demographics

One aspect that influences the development of burnout is the individual's personality traits and demographics. There are personality traits that make one more likely to burnout and there are personality traits that make one less likely to burnout. Also, your demographic makeup influences your likelihood to burnout. We will explore these components first.

An assumption that I had as I started researching was that HR professionals who had spent many years in their roles would be most likely to experience burnout. It struck me as counterintuitive that it was not those who had been in HR for many years who were most susceptible, but those who were new to their career. Studies show that burnout is very common amongst those new to their careers.[62] It makes a lot of sense when you think about it. Younger professionals have little control over their work. They are probably working hard to earn their place in the workforce, to earn their stripes, to make a name for themselves. They lack the resiliency that is built over a lengthy career. They are less likely to have the ability to take time off from work financially and earn fewer PTO hours, regardless of whether that

---

62 https://stress.lovetoknow.com/Which_Professionals_are_Prone_to_Burnout and https://www.growthbusiness.co.uk/jobs-likely-cause-burn-out-2550536/

is with paid time accrued or by taking unpaid time off. They also do not have the support networks and coping mechanisms that their senior colleagues will have. They are less likely to have developed the skills and finesse required to navigate highly political situations with ease. These factors combine together to lend themselves to burnout.

A similar factor is pay. Emolument found that employees earning more than 100,000 pounds a year experience the least burnout. Their research shows employees in lower paying roles experience burnout 90% of the time! They hypothesize that their resilience may have played a role in them obtaining these positions in the first place.[63] So, people who are more resilient are more likely to work in higher-paying roles. Higher pay would also allow for more freedom and flexibility over time. It also means they are more likely to be able to situate themselves financially to move into a different job if they are not satisfied in their current role. Generally speaking, higher pay usually means the employee has greater latitude for how the work is accomplished and more autonomy usually means less burnout.

Research also shows correlations between level of education and burnout frequency. Approximately 52% of those who hold Master's degrees experience burnout, Bachelor's degrees holders are around 71%, and those without a university degree are around 79% of the time.[64] The more education you possess the less likely you are to burnout. Some of this may be due to the correlation between degree and salary, too. They also posit that a degree offers the holder the opportunity to be more selective about their career and organization allowing degree-holders access to roles that are less likely to result in burnout as well as better options if they do begin to show the signs. This may also be because those with advanced degrees are doing less monotonous tasks.

It seems that the longer you remain employed, the more advantages that you have working in your favor. Your pay, resilience, responsibility,

---

63 https://www.growthbusiness.co.uk/jobs-likely-cause-burn-out-2550536/

64 https://www.growthbusiness.co.uk/jobs-likely-cause-burn-out-2550536

maturity, and flexibility tend to increase over your career. You have likely developed perspective and political savvy that help to serve you as you navigate difficult situations more skillfully. Furthermore, the Resilience Institute writes, “A consistent trend in our research shows that resilience is a learned skill that increases with age and experience.”[65] The older we get, the more able to deal with life circumstances we become.

Geography and culture also impact burnout. The United States is one of the least resilient cultures. We are average in reported fitness level and experienced flow state, and low in ability to focus, which would each serve in our favor for resilience if we were better off in these areas. We are average in feeling intensity and being self-critical and rank as the highest in worrying about the future, which furthermore detract from our resilience.[66] When you view the rankings of each country, you can see why we would rank low in resilience comparatively. We tend to be on the worst end of the spectrum in many traits.

Women occupy many HR positions and as is common with the glass ceiling, they tend to occupy lower positions within the HR function. Women have both physiological and familial/societal detractors that tend to work against us. Women tend to have lower resilience than men do overall.[67] They also commonly play greater roles in families as caretakers and bear more of the burden of raising children. This is particularly evident and crucial when the nuclear family is split.[68] It is not to say that men never have these roles, only that it is more common that women do. Women do have some interesting points working in their favor, too. “Women score

---

65 https://2krnrx3k2ieq4dsbl743vvpn-wpengine.netdna-ssl.com/wp-content/uploads/2018/08/Resilience-Enables-Strategic-Agility-2018.pdf

66 https://2krnrx3k2ieq4dsbl743vvpn-wpengine.netdna-ssl.com/wp-content/uploads/2018/08/Resilience-Enables-Strategic-Agility-2018.pdf

67 https://2krnrx3k2ieq4dsbl743vvpn-wpengine.netdna-ssl.com/wp-content/uploads/2018/08/Resilience-Enables-Strategic-Agility-2018.pdf

68 https://2krnrx3k2ieq4dsbl743vvpn-wpengine.netdna-ssl.com/wp-content/uploads/2018/08/Resilience-Enables-Strategic-Agility-2018.pdf

higher in positivity, insight, compassion, and connection."[69] Needless to say, each of us is unique in our demographic makeup and when we speak about demographics, we are speaking in generalities.

In addition to demographics, personality plays a significant role in determining your inclination for burnout. Personality traits that were mentioned repeatedly in the research that would encourage burnout include perfectionism, type A personalities, pessimism, emotional stability, low self-esteem, idealism, and sensitivity. Interestingly, I found that most of the respondents to the survey described themselves in positive terms in regards to personality. The descriptions used are also fairly stereotypical of HR professionals' personalities. Below is a word cloud of the most commonly used words HR professionals used to describe themselves:

69 https://2krnrx3k2ieq4dsbl743vvpn-wpengine.netdna-ssl.com/wp-content/uploads/2018/08/Resilience-Enables-Strategic-Agility-2018.pdf

We will walk through each of these components and compare the dimension with the profile of a typical (if there is such a thing) HR person.

In general, HR professionals tend to work in fairly thankless occupations that require a high level of detail. It is not generally acceptable to make errors where employee pay, benefits, communications, or terminations are concerned. We tend to hold ourselves to high standards. We see the work we do as important. Because of this, we are very achievement-oriented. Some research has indicated that overachievers have an increased predisposition to burnout.[70] Furthermore, perfectionism is linked to burnout. "Unhealthy perfectionism—fixation on flawless performance, dread of failure and obsessive approval seeking—predicts burnout."[71] Our need to always be seen as experts in our field and have all the answers puts a lot of pressure on us and can make us feel like failures when we are wrong. Every HR professional, except one, that I interviewed described themselves as a perfectionist. Worth noting, the one that did not describe herself as perfectionist appeared to be the happiest in her role and the least concerned about burnout. That does not seem to be a coincidence to me. I think it would be fair to say that lowering our perfect expectations of ourselves and allowing ourselves to be human, as we allow employees to be human, would be beneficial for us.

Type A personality classification is another factor linked to burnout. "[A]cting 'Type A' is related to emotional exhaustion, higher burnout levels and reduced job satisfaction."[72] Almost all of the interviews I conducted described themselves as Type A. If we are honest, to get things done in our organizations, we often have to be forceful. It is common in HR to have pretty thick skin and not shy away from sharing our insights about how to approach issues in a straightforward manner. HR is often put in the crosshairs of some of the organization's most complicated issues. This role could play into our burnout. It is tiring to share ideas and have them dismissed, especially if you consider yourself Type A. On the other hand,

70 https://www.tlnt.com/c-level-burnout-a-problem-no-one-talks-about/

71 https://www.psychologytoday.com/us/blog/the-gen-y-guide/201705/when-youre-tapped-age-30

72 https://www.psychologytoday.com/us/blog/the-gen-y-guide/201705/when-youre-tapped-age-30

some of us have achieved the coveted "seat at the table" and are respected.

Pessimism is highly correlated with burnout. "Above all, pessimism is the most closely and frequently associated [personality trait] with burnout."[73] Most of the HR professionals I talked to indicated that they were realistic or very optimistic. It may be that they were reluctantly reporting themselves as optimistic, and they did not feel so. This could also play into why we are burning out in such high numbers. Optimism is listed as one of the factors that increases resilience according to the Resilience Institute.[74] This is likely linked to a concept called self-efficacy, which is possibly the contributing variable. Self-efficacy is your confidence in your ability to exert control over your motivation, behavior, and social environment.

This could have a reducing effect on burnout, allowing HR professionals to ward it off for longer. The other possibility is that we could be self-reporting as optimistic when we do worry a lot about the negative possibilities. We are responsible for mitigating risk within our organizations, and it would be hard to do that without thinking of concerns.

Closely linked to pessimism is emotional stability. Being considered emotionally unstable is probably a tough pill to swallow, but think about it this way instead, do you tend to overthink things and get stuck on negative thoughts and not let them go? That may be a little more relatable. "[R]umination: neurotic self-attentiveness and/or heavily emotion-oriented coping. One example of ruminating is dwelling on personal injustices. Teachers who ruminate report higher stress levels and burnout more frequently."[75] I think we would all agree that this behavior is mostly negative and futile. It is not an easy behavior to curb either. In the

---

73 https://www.psychologytoday.com/us/blog/the-gen-y-guide/201705/when-youre-tapped-age-30

74 https://2krnrx3k2ieq4dsbl743vvpn-wpengine.netdna-ssl.com/wp-content/uploads/2018/08/Resilience-Enables-Strategic-Agility-2018.pdf

75 https://www.psychologytoday.com/us/blog/the-gen-y-guide/201705/when-youre-tapped-age-30

interviews, we were approximately split in half, half of us tended to ruminate and half of us expressed that we did not.

Having low self-esteem increases your likelihood of burnout. This was a mixed bag of responses in my interviews, with the tendency leaning towards medium or high. A few of the interviews talked about how they have high self-esteem at work but lower self-esteem outside of work. We appear to run the gamut from extremely self-confident to pretty low opinions of ourselves. One really common sign of burnout is a lack of efficacy, a lack of belief in your abilities to complete your job effectively. If you have low self-esteem, it would be easy to lose confidence in your ability to be effective. It is not a stretch to see how you would go from that to burnout fairly quickly. One of the saddest patterns that I noticed during my interviews was an accomplished, talented HR professional doubting their abilities because of the burnout they had experienced. The effects of burnout appear to have long-standing impact.

Most of us feel called to do HR (73.6% to be exact, according to my research). It appears that committing to what you do helps to keep you healthy and may help to guard us against burnout.[76] Furthermore, those of us who feel called to be in the profession also experienced more emotional reward than others according to my survey. It is not a huge surprise to see that those who are doing the work they felt they are meant to do, are more satisfied. The Resilience Institute lists apathy, which could be considered the opposite of having passion and commitment, to be one of the factors that decreases resilience.[77] Therefore, it is positive that most of us feel called to the HR profession since it appears that commitment to HR and being passionate about the field decreases your likelihood of burnout.

On the other hand, not being authentic is not good for us. "One study found that incongruence between implicit and explicit motives decreases wellbeing." This concept is also known as cognitive dissonance. The article

---

76 https://www.psychologytoday.com/us/blog/the-gen-y-guide/201705/when-youre-tapped-age-30

77 https://2krnrx3k2ieq4dsbl743vvpn-wpengine.netdna-ssl.com/wp-content/uploads/2018/08/Resilience-Enables-Strategic-Agility-2018.pdf

goes on to say that if you are pretending to be something you are not, "your burnout will call your bluff." [78] Masquerading or being forced to act like something you are not is not healthy.

Consider the story of Magic Johnson stepping down from his position as the president of the Los Angeles Lakers. Johnson alluded to the challenges he had faced trying to pretend to be something he was not. Mark Murphy, the author of the article, shared his study of 5,000 people. Respondents to his study who had to "put on a show" were 32% less likely to love what they did and if you didn't have to were 59% more likely to dislike their job.[79] Having to hide your emotions in HR is extremely common. We are expected to maintain utmost professionalism at difficult times. We are forced to hide our emotions and show empathy and concern when that may not be our true feelings. We often have to mask our true feelings for the sake of professionalism. Some of us have managed to bring our true, authentic selves to work successfully.

From the history of burnout, we know that many of the human services professionals fall victim to burnout because of their thwarted idealism. "It may be that while naive idealism magnifies one's vulnerability to burnout, it is not an essential prerequisite."[80] Possessing an idealistic view is not necessary for burnout to occur but can definitely encourage burnout. I think many of us initially joined HR because we wanted to help others. We get into the field and realize that we do not get to help employees the way we originally pictured. It can be disconcerting to revise your entire dream of how you saw your professional goals being achieved and where you saw your career heading. It is a disillusionment that does not occur overnight and can feel like it weighs upon your soul.

I believe there is a connection between sensitivity and burnout. In order to burnout, I firmly believe a person would need to give a shit. Ergo, those

---

78 https://www.psychologytoday.com/us/blog/the-gen-y-guide/201705/when-youre-tapped-age-30

79 https://www.forbes.com/sites/markmurphy/2019/04/10/magic-johnson-quitting-is-living-proof-of-this-study-that-faking-emotions-at-work-can-cause-misery/?ss=leadershipstrategy#4b91dd194248

80 https://www.wilmarschaufeli.nl/publications/Schaufeli/311.pdf

who are sensitive, passionate, and take their work seriously are more likely to burnout. This concept is known as conscientiousness in psychology. It is unfortunate that caring can become a weakness in this regard. On the flip side, having compassion can also work in your favor and make you less susceptible to burnout. HR is a profession that tends to attract people who genuinely want to see the best for the people that they serve. This concern and caring may be a factor in our burnout.

I also believe that many HR professionals could be categorized as Laura Empson's "insecure overachievers" model, incredibly self-motivated, driven, and hard-working individuals who may be particularly prone to burnout:

> Insecure overachievers are exceptionally capable and fiercely ambitious, yet driven by a profound sense of their own inadequacy. This typically stems from childhood, and may result from various factors, such as experience of financial or physical deprivation, or a belief that their parents' love was contingent upon their behaving and performing well...
>
> Paradoxically, the professionals I studied still believe that they have autonomy and that they are overworking by choice. They do not blame their organizations, which after all have invested in work-life balance initiatives and wellness programs. Instead, they blame themselves for being inadequate. Their colleagues seem to be coping, and they take that as further evidence of their own inadequacy. They do not talk honestly to their colleagues about their problems, thus perpetuating the myth of the invincible professional, which encourages their colleagues to feel inadequate in turn. If they suffer burnout, they think it is their fault. Their organization and its leadership are

> absolved of responsibility, so nothing fundamental changes.[81]

I am not saying that all HR professionals match this description, only that it sounds familiar to me. Of course we have to prove ourselves. Of course we have to work all of these hours to get the work done. There is no way we, the HR professionals, could be burned out; we are responsible for helping others with burnout, so we must deny it in ourselves!

The Resilience Institute's Resilience Enable Strategic Agility: Global Resilience Report 2018 outlines six factors that will decrease resilience and six factors that will increase resilience: [82]

| Decrease Resilience: | Increase Resilience: |
|---|---|
| Apathy | Assertiveness |
| Disconnect | Decisiveness |
| Hostility | Focus |
| Joylessness | Fulfillment |
| Rumination | Optimism |
| Sadness | Presence |

Kaschka et al. suggests the following additional internal factors or personality traits that may drive burnout:

- *High (idealistic) expectations of self, high ambition, perfectionism*
- *Strong need for recognition*
- *Always wanting to please other people, suppressing own needs*
- *Feeling irreplaceable; not wanting/able to delegate*
- *Hard work and commitment to the point of overestimation of self and becoming overburdened*
- *Work as the only meaningful activity, work as substitute for social life*[83]

---

81 https://captainawkward.com/2019/05/08/1198-how-do-i-deal-with-work-burnout-and-make-my-partner-happy-my-partner-my-boss-who-is-a-partner-in-the-law-firm-where-i-work/

82 https://2krnrx3k2ieq4dsbl743vvpn-wpengine.netdna-ssl.com/wp-content/uploads/2018/11/Resilience-Enables-Strategic-Agility-2018.pdf

83 https://www.ncbi.nlm.nih.gov/pmc/articles/PMC3230825/

From my impressions, HR professionals tend to possess these positive traits: passion (not apathetic), deeply connected, little hostility (overall a fairly professional group), moderate happiness, moderate assertiveness, fairly decisive, moderate focus, somewhat fulfilled, and self-reporting as optimistic. Our negative personality traits include a tendency to ruminate, be perfectionists, be people pleasers, not being able to let go of our job duties, and overloading ourselves, and some lack assertiveness, decisiveness, and focus, and over time, we can become irritable, unfulfilled and disconnected, if we experience burnout.

HR professionals tend to be fairly resilient and have many positive traits. I think overall we have faced our numerous challenges with admirable bravery. Our resiliency might mean that it may take us longer to burnout. I do think that this resilience to burnout means that when burnout occurs, it is more spectacular. I also believe that many of us have been secretly feeling burned out for quite some time and were not sure how to approach these feelings or have been denying them. For me, reading through the personality traits and seeing how my own personality is impacting my burnout was eye-opening. I can see a lot of myself in these descriptions.

# Oxygen: Environment

Burnout can come from environmental factors both at work or outside work. Because burnout is considered a work-related problem, we are going to focus the majority of this section's discussion on work-related and only briefly touch on our home lives and their potential impact at the end of this section. "According to Statistic Brain, the number one cause of stress in American adults is job pressure."[84] Over and over again, I found that work is the number one stressor in most adult lives. It is also costing the economy in astronomical ways. "According to an article by Harvard Business School Working Knowledge, workplace stress caused extra expenditures of anywhere from $125 to $190 billion a year in healthcare

---

84 https://www.forbes.com/sites/alankohll/2017/07/19/7-ways-to-avoid-hr-burnout/1

costs."[85] Between the emotional and financial costs, it is important that we understand how our stress at work is contributing to burnout.

There are a number of factors that can be attributed to our external environments. Kaschka et al. suggests the following external factors:

- *High demands at work*
- *Problems of leadership and collaboration*
- *Contradictory instructions*
- *Time pressure*
- *Bad atmosphere at work; bullying*
- *Lack of freedom to make decisions*
- *Lack of influence on work organization*
- *Few opportunities to participate*
- *Low autonomy/right to contribute opinions*
- *Hierarchy problems*
- *Poor internal communication (employers, employees)*
- *Administrative constraints*
- *Pressure from superiors*
- *Increasing responsibility*
- *Poor work organization*
- *Lack of resources (personnel, funding)*
- *Problematic institutional rules and structures*
- *Lack of perceived opportunities for promotion*
- *Lack of clarity about roles*
- *Lack of positive feedback*
- *Poor teamwork*
- *Absence of social support*

This is a great framework to start with. Work environments have changed rapidly in recent years. Organizations have become more globalized and culturally diverse. Technology changes constantly. This progression has allowed us to always be connected but also means that we feel as though we are always on and need to be readily available at any second. Irene McConnell attributes the top three causes of burnout to work overload, powerlessness, and insufficient reward.[86] The rising workload is having a

85 https://www.forbes.com/sites/alankohll/2017/07/19/7-ways-to-avoid-hr-burnout/1

86 https://www.tlnt.com/c-level-burnout-a-problem-no-one-talks-about/

pronounced effect on employees' wellbeing. "Employees with large caseloads experience burnout more often."[87] Logically, the more you have on your plate, the more likely you are to experience burnout. Overload alone is not enough to cause burnout, and it usually requires an ongoing period of overload. One colleague shared during an interview that her stress stemmed from unrealistic demands. She gave an example that she was told to close all current job openings by the end of the year and that senior team especially wanted the jobs closed from the system within two weeks. She remarked that there was a general lack of understanding of what happened once the offer is made, there are pre-screening processes and sometimes notice periods that push out start dates, making these dates almost unachievable. She felt the stress on her to get the work done in this unreasonable time frame.

We are expected to be more productive than ever and work pace is faster today than it has ever been. Everyone is trying to do more with less. Working hours and workloads have steadily risen. It is not uncommon today for organizations to conduct layoffs, which result in considerable stress both for employees and to some extent especially for HR staff. HR is often brought in on these decisions beforehand, which can result in challenging situations as you try to keep the layoff confidential from people who you care about. Mergers and acquisitions are another common source of stress and challenge for organizations and for HR professionals. These are becoming more frequent, both overall and at times repeating within the same organization. They dramatically add to the workload in HR.

Interestingly, burnout appears to be more prevalent the larger the organization is. In organizations with 100-500 employees, HR professionals considered burnout to be the cause of 10 percent or less of their turnover while in organizations of 2,500 plus, they indicated that they anticipated that burnout was responsible for 50 percent or more.[88] One possible explanation is that HR in smaller organizations are spread more thinly,

---

87 https://www.psychologytoday.com/us/blog/the-gen-y-guide/201705/when-youre-tapped-age-30

88 https://www.kronos.com/about-us/newsroom/employee-burnout-crisis-study-reveals-big-workplace-challenge-2017

resulting in less awareness of the issue that burnout is creating. Smaller organizations may also have less burnout because employees are valued and seen more as individuals rather than "as a number." It may be difficult for an employee in a smaller organization to experience burnout without someone taking notice and offering assistance before the employee leaves the organization.

Overall, employment has changed drastically in the last few decades. It used to be that once you were hired with an organization, you would rarely switch organizations. You might move up over time, but loyalty was common and benefited both parties. I believe the lack of loyalty started on the organizations' end, due to economic conditions resulting in layoffs. Previously, an employee's loyalty had meant retirement, possibly including a pension and a gold watch. When layoffs became widespread, that loyalty was shattered and employees chose to look out for themselves. Regardless of the reason, neither employees nor organizations exhibit the same loyalty today, which results in more frequent job changes. Changing jobs can be stressful. Learning a new organization with different rules and politics is exhausting. In comparison, it is much less strenuous and easier to remain with the same organization where you know what to expect.

Perhaps one of the most difficult things for employees that lead to burnout is reconciling the organization's stated values and their actual values. "Employees exercise severe judgment when they witness a gap between organizational intentions and reality."[89] It causes employees to question the organization and their place in it as well as how they will be treated by the organization. I think this is a very common cause of burnout, even by well-meaning organizations. These changes within organizations overall pose specific challenges for HR professionals. HR is in a unique and sometimes difficult position caught in between employees and management's needs. Many view us as an advocate for employees while also needing to keep the businesses' needs in mind. Balancing both of these needs at the same time can seem impossible. HR is also frequently caught up in situations where the stated values misalign with practiced

---

89 https://www.wilmarschaufeli.nl/publications/Schaufeli/311.pdf

values and that can create struggles for employees as well as the HR professional.

The difference between the idealism and reality of what helping people actually looks like in HR poses challenges similar to human services professionals as their profession emerged. Many of us actively sought out this profession because we wanted to make a difference. Unfortunately, that dream does not sync up with the real world, especially when we are first starting out. Sometimes our employers do not empower us to reach our true potential and capabilities. Sometimes helping an employee means separating them from a position that is not a fit for them, despite how difficult that is. Sometimes we are disparaged by the employees that we are trying to help because they are angry and do not understand our role.

Research shows that as long as we find our work to have meaning we are less likely to burnout. Professor Ayala Malach-Pines writes, "The root cause of burnout lies in people's need to believe that their lives are meaningful, that the things they do are useful and important. For many people, the driving force behind their work is not merely monetary but the belief that they can have an impact, and it is this idea that spurs them on…it is possible to be very stressed but not burned out if you feel your work is worthwhile and you are achieving the desired goals."[90] HR is a job that is difficult but also directly affects employees in a number of positive ways. Losing sight of this is one possible cause of our burnout. It is also difficult that few appreciate what we do for the organization and much of our work is behind the scenes.

Our jobs continue to expand as we come up with additional insights into what drives employee behavior and we conceive of new projects to drive value in our organizations. "HR professionals have a lot on their plates. Wearing multiple hats and dealing with tight deadlines throughout the year can lead to a lot of built-up stress and negative energy."[91] There is not a slow time of year for most of us. We recruit all year round. We have an

---

90 Rise and Shine: Recover from burnout and get back to your best.

91 https://www.forbes.com/sites/alankohll/2017/07/19/7-ways-to-avoid-hr-burnout/1

open enrollment season, end of the year payroll, and annual reports, and affirmative action plans due. There is no timing of investigations, which happen when they happen and require our urgent attention. If your roles are anything like mine have been, there are times of the year where I am the busiest, and the rest of the year I am just busy.

Burnout is also common in positions that are people-centric.[92] HR is heavily people-oriented work. Very few days do not require extensive interaction with others in our jobs. Burnout is also particularly common in helping professions, such as human services, healthcare, etc. "Customer facing occupations also pay a toll for employer mandated emotional labor."[93] Generally speaking, our customers are our employees. HR bears the brunt of much of the emotional labor of our employees. We can see them at their worst: terminations, deaths, divorces, loss of benefits, emotional situations requiring EAPs, when addiction issues arise, and when performance requires documentation. We essentially take on the emotional work of our employees and our employers. It is not uncommon that we do not get breaks and frequently we are stopped by an employee outside of work to answer a quick question. When was the last time you attempted to sit down in a breakroom and take a break at work?

Two of the top causes of stress amongst physicians are regulatory compliance and internal bureaucracy, two things that HR professionals are inundated with as well. The report goes on to say, "The underlying theme from physicians' main areas of frustration was anything that takes time and attention away from them treating their patients."[94] You probably did not seek out this field because you wanted to deal with compliance or internal politics. How much of your time is dedicated to these items now? How much of your time is spent on paperwork and less value-add work? Now think about how much of your time you spend doing what you truly excel at and what those tasks look like. Many of us may not see a lot of similarity

---

92 https://www.psychologytoday.com/us/blog/the-gen-y-guide/201705/when-youre-tapped-age-30

93 https://www.quora.com/What-professions-do-you-feel-have-the-highest-incidences-of-burnout-and-why

94 https://www.reactiondata.com/report/physician-burnout/

between those two separate functions. The compliance and bureaucracy we face can take us away from serving what we feel is most important: our employees.

Many of the organizational pressures today are ones that HR is considered responsible for. Paula Davis-Laack writes, "At work, there is decreased wellbeing, lower staff retention, higher organizational system costs, higher turnover rates, lower morale and lack of cohesion in the organization as a whole."[95] Each of these factors directly affect HR on an almost daily basis. We do not necessarily have control over them entirely, but they are functions that we are seen as impacting. As these concerns grow in our organizations, the pressure to overcome them can become overwhelming for us.

In addition, many of us suffer from stress from our home lives too. Dr. Jeanine Joy is the founder of the Happiness 1st Institute and has authored books on burnout. She indicates that "[s]tress from the occupation is one part of the equation, stress from home can add to the risk or, if the home is a healthy supportive environment, it can add support that delays or prevents burnout."[96] My research showed that having a good family life and support network was connected to reduced burnout. In other words, when our home life is good, it can mean that we are less prone to burnout, but if our home life is not good, it can result in a greater likelihood of burnout. The most common stresses experienced at home are usually centered around time, relationships, politics, and financial issues. Here is a word cloud of the most common words used to describe HR professional's main stressors outside of work:

---

95 https://www.tlnt.com/c-level-burnout-a-problem-no-one-talks-about/

96 https://www.quora.com/What-professions-do-you-feel-have-the-highest-incidences-of-burnout-and-why

## Fuel: Stress/Critical Events

Eventually, personality and environment combine with stressful events culminating in burnout. Caroline Beaton writes in her article *When You're Tapped Before Age 30*, "Burnout is weakly correlated to stressful events."[97] Weakly correlated, does not mean much, right? Stressful events are likely a mediating variable, meaning in order for them to have an impact, it must be in the presence of other variables, such as personality and environment. Therefore, in the right circumstances, a stressful event is unlikely to cause burnout, because it is more of a chronic than acute problem. I think that is because the personality/demographic traits and environment have to be conducive to burnout as well in order for the stressful event to cause burnout. We all have experienced stress and it does not always result in burnout. If the conditions for personality and environment are right, adding the right stress will result in burnout.

So what are potential events that could contribute to burnout? The main issues I uncovered were time/workload, management, incivility, reward, and personal matters. These factors could potentially impact any profession, and this will include both general discussion of these issues and

---

97 https://www.psychologytoday.com/us/blog/the-gen-y-guide/201705/when-youre-tapped-age-30

also how they are most likely to impact HR. Here is a word cloud of the most commonly used words describing what caused HR professionals' burnout:

All of us realize when we have bitten off more than we can chew in our professional and personal lives. You probably know the feeling well: not being sure when you are going to get everything done, feeling stressed out, and overwhelmed. I believe that most of us also recognize there is an issue with being overworked in our roles, but we are too busy to do something about it. There was one survey response that I think captured this particularly well. When asked if the respondent was willing to conduct an interview to share more perspective, he or she responded with, "No, that just adds more to the plate and more stress." We are so burned out that we cannot even be bothered to take the time to understand our own burnout! We are inundated with work while at the office and we fill our personal lives with so much that we have little downtime. I know for me, there were times when I was so caught up in getting the next task completed that I did not have time to strategically plan my work, let alone think about my current mental state.

I think that previously experiencing burnout predisposes you to additional cases of burnout, similar to heat stroke. Unless you take the steps necessary to rectify what caused you to be burned out in the first place, it makes you more susceptible for the next round. "Another study showed that burnout at the baseline predicted increased fatigue four years later, and the reverse was also observed."[98] Once you experience burnout, you are going to be weakened for a period of time. Personally, I believe this happens because we do not resolve the issues that were causing us to be burned out in the first place, we only heal enough so we can keep performing. It is almost like a cumulative trauma disorder, where each repeated blow creates more damage, until a final blow renders you unable to function. Perhaps you have found a way to put a band-aid on the problem and relieve the symptoms, but without resolving the underlying causes, you are going to keep ending up burned out again.

HR is often viewed as the department that helps the organization deal with burnout. It often falls under HR's purview to coach employees through burnout. How can we possibly admit that we have burnout ourselves and maintain our expertise in this area? We also cannot accept the possibility that we too could become burned out. It is viewed negatively in our society to say that we are so exhausted that it is impacting our ability to perform. It is still taboo to play the burnout card. Praseea Nair writes, "[m]oreover, stigma attached to burn-outs is likely to deal such a blow to a top performing professional's career that they are unlikely to thrive should they recover and return to their teams[.]"[99]

In my experience, it was difficult for me to begin researching this at first. I was concerned about what others would think, or worse yet, what my employer or potential future employers might think of me researching HR burnout! I remember when my manager called me into his office and showed me that he had found my website and had been looking at it. We both had a good laugh. I was fortunate that my manager was fairly understanding and had a good sense of humor, but not all of us are so

98 https://www.wilmarschaufeli.nl/publications/Schaufeli/481.pdf

99 https://www.growthbusiness.co.uk/jobs-likely-cause-burn-out-2550536/

lucky. While it ended well, I felt like I was disclosing my burnout. There was a certain amount of shame and uncertainty involved.

A similar issue was mentioned regarding CEO's burnout: denial. "The NeuroBusiness Group study focused mostly on male CEOs, with each of them describing wanting to 'power through' their stress."[100] This was also listed as a method for firefighters who experienced burnout.[101] Trying to deny that you are feeling burned out and pushing through it instead can create negative effects that could haunt you for a lifetime. Many HR professionals may feel pressure to work through their own challenges too, especially considering that their CEOs may have displayed that attitude. It may mean that a problem that is fairly small will be exacerbated, resulting in a longer recovery time. Denial can prevent you from getting the help that you need for your burnout. If you are unfamiliar with the signs, you may gloss over how you are feeling and eventually end up in a much worse place then if you had proactively dealt with it.

Another issue that is mentioned as frequently contributing to burnout is workplace incivility. Incivility is defined as "behaviors that demonstrate lack of regard for others in the workplace, described as rude or discourteous."[102] Incivility is becoming a rampant epidemic within some of our organizations. Christine Porath's research found that almost 50% of people surveyed in 1998 experienced incivility at least once a month, which increased to 55% in 2011, and again to 62% in 2016.[103] Unfortunately, the pervasiveness is quickly rising. In HR, 63.6% of respondents reported experiencing incivility at least once a month according to my research. Another fascinating piece of data my research showed was that incivility and burnout were correlated. If you witness incivility, you are more likely

---

100 https://www.tlnt.com/c-level-burnout-a-problem-no-one-talks-about/

101 https://scholarworks.umt.edu/cgi/viewcontent.cgi?referer=https://www.google.com/&httpsredir=1&article=1454&context=etd

102 http://www.na-businesspress.com/AJM/DoshyPV_Web14_1-2_.pdf

103 https://www.mckinsey.com/business-functions/organization/our-insights/the-hidden-toll-of-workplace-incivility

to burnout. Furthermore, the frequency of incivility and health were negatively correlated; as people suffer more incivility, their health suffers too! This could leave you susceptible to burnout or to other medical issues.

Incivility ranges from mild behavior such as casually ignoring someone during a meeting for a few moments to check an email or poking fun at someone while joking around to more serious offenses such as name-calling or ignoring a co-worker's requests resulting in lowered productivity. During her interview, a colleague shared that while many employees were overall respectful, some downright lacked that respect and would speak to her in harsh, demanding tones. Her immediate response was to stop them and say, "Hold on a second, I want to help you, but we need to respect one another." It seemed employees had forgotten that we are on the same team and are co-workers and there are professional norms to be respected. While some of these examples seem fairly innocuous, according to Porath, "small uncivil actions can lead to much bigger problems, like aggression and violence," if they are left unchecked.[104] In fact, Doshy, et. al, indicates that there is a spiral effect to incivility. Stress causes employees to be uncivil, causing more stress and further incivility.[105] It becomes a vicious cycle of stress and incivility. Allowing incivility in the first place can cause worsening incivility and potentially other issues within the organization, such as challenges with recruiting and employee relations issues, which ultimately affect HR as well.

Porath outlines all sorts of negative effects of incivility, including lowered motivation and productivity and performance, lost time, and turnover.[106] I think allowing a culture of incivility will also create a culture where people are more susceptible to burnout. Obviously, when reviewing the effects of incivility, it is easy to imagine an environment where this is occurring not being an ideal environment. Furthermore, I hypothesize that incivility in the workplace affects HR more than it affects other employees. HR is more likely to have to address issues that come up due to incivility and therefore

---

104 https://www.youtube.com/watch?v=py4P8b4t3DI

105 http://www.na-businesspress.com/AJM/DoshyPV_Web14_1-2_.pdf

106 https://www.youtube.com/watch?v=py4P8b4t3DI

to be exposed to any instances of incivility. Porath's research found decreases in performance even in witnesses.[107] Who witnesses more incivility in organizations than the HR department? When you think of all the negative effects of incivility, imagine all the negative implications for us in our roles: emotional burdens, increased workloads, lower organizational efficiency, etc.

Incivility also decreases job satisfaction. In fact, Doshy indicates that it is "[o]ne of the most widely cited constructs...[a]s incivility rose, job satisfaction declined."[108] This is a logical correlation. Who wants to go to work every day and be treated poorly? Whose job satisfaction would not suffer? Then, turnover increases and absenteeism increases and HR is responsible for hiring more employees to help to cover the work that is not being covered due to incivility. The negative effects on HR of incivility continue to pile up. We also dedicate our time to trying to resolve these issues, which pulls us away from other valuable work we could be doing and exposes us to more incivility. Ultimately, incivility can also lead to major retention, recruiting, and succession planning issues.[109] Incivility is a huge issue in organizations and creates ongoing problems for HR.

In addition, many HR professionals do not feel like they are adequately rewarded for their work. Lack of appreciation was a very common theme. Many of us expressed that we do not feel listened to, wins are few and far between, managers are uncooperative, and overall we are not feeling valued. Over 75% of HR professionals responding to my survey indicated that they either did not feel emotionally rewarded for their work or only felt that way some of the time. There is no doubt that HR can be a very thankless job. You have to be motivated internally in this job, because the day-to-day of being in HR will wear you out if you cannot regenerate yourself. Positive moments where it feels like it is worth it can be few and far between. Also, many employees and managers have misconceptions about what HR is supposed to do and their role in the organization. This

---

107 https://www.youtube.com/watch?v=py4P8b4t3DI

108 https://files.eric.ed.gov/fulltext/ED501638.pdf

109 http://www.na-businesspress.com/AJM/DoshyPV_Web14_1-2_.pdf

can make achieving expectations difficult if not impossible and results in disappointed co-workers.

Life outside work can cause the stress necessary for burnout to ignite. These concerns can be financial, relationship, or time-related. Financial struggles are very common in our society. Student loans, bills, rising prices, and living at home were all mentioned as concerns by respondents to the survey. Society has an interesting relationship with money and the challenges posed continue to morph with each generation. Relationships also play a role in burnout, family stress being one of the most common. This can include spouses and significant others, children, and elderly parents. Some people cited a lack of support from their relationships as their biggest concern. There were many examples of the helpful types that ended up gravitating toward HR, who feel like they are always lending a helping hand and not receiving much support in return.

However, the most commonly cited personal issue mentioned was lack of available time. Lack of time resulted in not being able to complete self-care activities such as cleaning or exercising. It means we are not taking time to reflect on how we are doing currently. This is probably a particularly trying challenge for those who are extremely busy at work. I can say from personal experience, when I relocated to a small rural community from a city, my stress level declined immediately, from not having to deal with traffic twice every day. I did not realize how much pent-up frustration I would get from driving to and from work daily!

Overextending was also a common theme. We have taken on too much and can no longer meet all of our commitments. Some people also lamented that there wasn't enough time to be able to do everything that they would prefer to do. Collectively, we often take on too much. The growing number of hours spent working also eat into our personal time.

One thing that I wanted to look into during this research is why burnout is so taboo in HR. We seem almost ashamed to talk about it. Over and over again, I heard respondents say that the questions were interesting or that no one had ever asked them about this before. However, as we talked about burnout, people poured their hearts out with passion. Most of the people I reached out to, despite being busy and possibly burned out, were still willing and excited to discuss this.

I think one of the main causes of not being willing to discuss burnout more openly is we do not want to be seen as inferior or pegged as ineffective for becoming burned out ourselves. We are afraid that showing any weakness will reflect negatively on us. Could it be that we are covering up our burnout, like Praseeda Nair thinks bankers may be? "Stories of burn-outs in the banking sector are often found in the media, but, surprisingly, relatively few bankers declare having had a burn-out (56 per cent). Could it be that a macho banking culture, which glorifies hard work and 100-hour weeks, might discourage employees from acknowledging a burn-out?"[110] HR is not a "macho" culture, but there is definitely a glorification of being busy within HR. We take pride in working the most hours.

Perhaps we are pushing our burnout under the rug and trying to push through it? "The signs and symptoms of burnout are often highly visible, but they can be easy to ignore, particularly if you are working in an aggressive corporate culture where any sign of strain might be perceived as weakness or an inability to do the job."[111] I do not think HR is usually viewed as an "aggressive" department (although there are organizations and individuals that are the exceptions to every rule). Another possibility is that we are so busy that we are trying to get through the next task rather than reflecting upon our emotional needs, resulting in burnout being ignored. Regardless of what the reason is, in order for us to start doing some of the important work of healing our burnout, we are going to have to accept our current state, whatever that may be, and openly talk about the issues we experience and how to tackle them. I know denying the truth and burying my head under a mountain of tasks played a role in my own burnout. The importance of taking a step back and surveying your current situation and taking active steps based on that information cannot be understated. It is crucial for our own wellbeing.

---

110 https://www.growthbusiness.co.uk/jobs-likely-cause-burn-out-2550536/

111 Rise and Shine: Recover from burnout and get back to your best.

This chapter has been an overview of how personality and demographics combine with environmental factors and are ignited by a stressful event culminating in burnout. Similar to a fire, all three of these elements must be present in adequate quantities in order to result in burnout.

ঌ৵

# HR Burnout – The Experience

*Come on, baby, light my fire, try to set the night on fire.*
The Doors

I could fill a book with anecdotes from the field about HR burnout. As I started researching this topic for my own personal knowledge, it boggled my mind how common I found the experience. As I discussed with colleagues the feelings and emotions I was having, they would share their similar stories of what they were experiencing. Eventually, it became too much of a distinct pattern for me to ignore and I knew I had to obtain a deeper understanding. Not all of us experience burnout, but it is unfortunately common in HR. With each conversation, I would only have more questions and there did not appear to be good answers.

Burnout tends to present itself in stages and does not occur all at once. Bella Zanesco, CEO of Wellboard, even proposes a stage of burnout known as "brownout" where you first start to feel the symptoms of burnout.[112] Her model views burnout as a seven-stage process:

1. Frustration
2. Anger
3. Apathy
4. Burnout
5. Withdrawal
6. Self-knowledge/acceptance
7. Recovery

Not all people experience all of these stages and it is possible to experience them out of this order or have multiple stages at one time. It is important

112 https://www.tlnt.com/c-level-burnout-a-problem-no-one-talks-about/

to catch burnout early on and take steps to prevent further issues as it can have some extreme, long-lasting effects otherwise. For example, Alexandra Michel writes in *Burnout and the Brain*, "Research from an integrative team of psychological scientists at the Karolinska Institute in Sweden provides striking evidence that workplace burnout can alter neural circuits, ultimately causing a vicious cycle of neurological dysfunction."[113] Basically, burnout can rewire your brain. Alexandra also refers to a study showing that those with burnout had more sensitive reactions than healthy people, indicating that burnout may cause us to be more sensitive, weakening our ability to react in a healthy manner. Science of People indicates that burnout can influence moodiness, cognitive functioning, learning ability, creativity, memory, problem solving skills, and attention.[114] This could have effects on your ability, in and out of work. Burnout over time can be very serious and can lead to long-term health problems. Ultimately, it could even lead to death in extreme cases if you do not take action. Think of the Japanese karoshi.

Ingrid Vaughan, an HR Manager, shared her poignant version of her own burnout. It was extremely vulnerable and forthcoming and sheds light on how we feel about our burnout. Ingrid reports that when she came forward to a medical professional about her burnout, the medical professional recommended taking off work immediately. Ingrid said she had a "deeply rooted fear of inadequacy—of people thinking [her] incompetent."[115] With her time off at her cabin, she started off by resting for a significant period of time and as she started recovering, she read, wrote, and talked about her experience. She did a lot of work around uncovering unhealthy modes of thinking and working on ways that she could improve her life going forward. "People often think of burnout only as it relates to work overload, but I believe it can happen when the combined stresses of life supersede your emotional and physical capacity to cope."[116] Ingrid says that because of her experience she has an incredible understanding of the effect that

---

113 https://www.psychologicalscience.org/observer/burnout-and-the-brain

114 https://www.scienceofpeople.com/burnout/

115 https://www.heretohelp.bc.ca/visions/workplace-vol9/to-the-brink-and-back

116 https://www.heretohelp.bc.ca/visions/workplace-vol9/to-the-brink-and-back

burnout has in others and is quick to recognize burnout. The experience has helped her and given her greater sensitivity to what others experience. She recommends taking steps to get the time off you need from work and ways to best coordinate this. She also suggests being very open with your employer and your support network. This step certainly requires bravery but she outlines how this was essential for her recovery.

From my personal experience, losing my position and being forced to move and leave my commitments and network behind was very difficult to do but eye-opening as to how much I had taken on. At one point, I was working a full-time job, completing my Master's degree, starting a DisruptHR chapter, and trying to enjoy some semblance of a social life. When I moved, I was still working a full-time job (that I had just started, so it required a little more dedication to begin with), but I had completed my Master's degree and lost all the social and volunteer commitments that I previously had. I was awed with all the free time I suddenly had. I understand that my situation is different from most and that would be difficult to replicate. I was unmarried, no children, and with me and my cat to worry about, it became obvious that I had been overextended previously. I was finally able to take some time for myself, focus on my health, and read for my own enjoyment again. I relished the opportunity to take a step back and reinvent my life to focus on what was important to me.

So, how do you know if you have HR burnout? I have included the following questions to help you start assessing your own burnout. This is a fairly exhaustive list and I am not including a key. However, when you are done reading the questions, you will likely assess that you are doing fine or that you have something to address. Trust your gut instinct. It is better to be safe than sorry. Seek professional help immediately if you are concerned. The remaining chapters will also provide recommendations and suggestions.

- Physical symptoms
    - Has your diet changed?
    - Do you feel exhausted?

    - Has your sleep suffered?
    - Are you experiencing physical symptoms (headaches, unexplained soreness, stomach problems, etc.)?
    - Have you been drinking more alcohol than usual?
    - Have you neglected your self-care?
    - Do you have time for the things you enjoy?
- Emotional symptoms
    - Do you feel depressed or anxious?
    - Do you consider yourself to be more sensitive than usual?
    - Are you cynical?
    - Are you more critical than usual?
    - Do you suffer from apathy?
    - Do you feel emotionally exhausted?
    - Are you irritable?
    - Are you isolating yourself?
    - Do you feel sad, frazzled, hopeless, or disengaged?
    - Have you been experiencing more mood swings than usual?
    - Do you feel more aggressive than usual?
    - Do you feel despair?
    - Do you feel more likely to cry than usual?
    - Do you feel less committed than usual?
    - Have your reactions to others felt out of character lately?
    - Have you had unusually strong emotional reactions to events?
    - Have you found yourself convincing yourself there is not a problem?
    - Have you been socially withdrawn?
    - Have you felt empty lately?
    - Do you obsess about work while not there?
- Motivation symptoms
    - Has your productivity dropped?
    - Have you missed more work than usual lately?
    - Do you find that there are periods of time at work where you cannot bring yourself to be productive?

    - Do you struggle to find meaning from your work?
    - Do you feel overworked?
    - Do you feel committed to your organization's mission?
    - Have you felt an increased pressure to meet your goals?
    - Have you felt reduced commitment to the employee populations you serve or your work?
    - Have you struggled to focus lately?
    - Do you feel you lack direction?
- Symptoms at work
    - Do you feel you have to distance yourself from work in order to continue?
    - Have you been working more than usual?
    - Are you checking emails compulsively when you are not at work?
    - Have you been working more on the weekends?
    - Has your work's quality suffered?
    - Have you forgotten things?
    - Have you missed deadlines?
    - Are you more prone to making mistakes than usual?
    - Are you more prone to blaming others than usual?
    - Has your creativity suffered?
    - Have you made what you feel are bad decisions lately?
    - Do you feel less mentally on point than usual?
    - Do you feel you are rewarded for your work financially?
    - Do you feel you are rewarded for your work emotionally?
    - Do you think your organization treats you well?
    - Do you have the tools you need to do your job?
    - Does your manager support you?
    - Does your manager have the ability to do anything about the areas where you need additional support?
    - Have you thought of leaving the profession?

I think most of us probably emerge from this activity with a pretty good understanding of where we are sitting presently. It is not important that you diagnose burnout during this exercise. What is important is that if you determine that you have a problem, that you are aware of it and that you have some resources to address it. Would you like to try out the most widely known burnout inventory as well? The Maslach Burnout Inventory is also included as an appendix to this book. The original MBI form had 22 questions that were divided into three categories: emotional exhaustion, depersonalization, and personal accomplishment.[117] It is important that we take the time to reflect on our current situation and how we are doing at this moment. I know this is a valuable exercise for me and is often evident if I take the time to think about it.

117 https://www.ncbi.nlm.nih.gov/pmc/articles/PMC3230825/

# Withdrawal – The End

*I fell into a burning ring of fire. I went down down down and the flames went higher.*

Johnny Cash

Eventually, if the situation continues to deteriorate and never improves, the stress compounds and the end result can be withdrawal. Withdrawal can take a variety of forms: disengagement in your current role, time off, or a career change or altogether ceasing to seek employment of any kind. In fact, 45% of respondents to the survey I conducted indicated that they had considered leaving HR due to burnout. As mentioned previously, burnout can be so severe that it could lead to death. Burnout has the potential to consume and impact your entire life in massive ways. Looking at leaving a position or the profession overall has far-reaching effects on more than your career.

Our financial health, important health and other benefits, social connections, and sense of self are all closely tied to our employment. Burnout is a challenge because you are fighting to hang onto your job that provides you with resources to sustain your life, while it may be causing you harm.

Most of us need to work. We need our jobs for the income and benefits derived from them. We feel obligated to maintain our jobs so that we can continue to earn income. Being in a situation where you know that what is best for you would be to quit and walk away from your job and knowing that you cannot do that because you need the paycheck may be one of the worst feelings in the world.

We also derive a lot of our social contact from work. Anyone who has been laid off or let go from a job knows that when you do not have to get up in the morning and go to work, it gets lonely very quickly. Most of us spend more time each day with our co-workers than we do with our friends or family. It is common to spend more time at work than in any other single activity. It can be very difficult to envision leaving our jobs and the people that we support, even voluntarily, even when we know that it may be best. Every job has people that you like and then those that you could probably do without. It is very rare that an organization has no good people at all! The thought of having to break it to the people that you support that you are experiencing burnout and need to take time off to take care of yourself (gasp!) is enough to cause many of us severe anxiety.

It is also common that we associate our identity with our work. How often do you approach someone new and within the first five minutes of conversation know what they do for a living? It is often one of the first distinguishing characteristics we long to uncover. We identify as our career of choice. We commit to it, dedicating ourselves to proficiency in it. We take a lot of pride in it. We work hard to climb that career ladder. We know that our financial and social status depend on us being successful. In HR, it is a particularly inescapable truth as we go around discussing performance management, reviews, and discipline. How well you do your job will directly affect your quality of life. This makes it that much harder to admit that we are experiencing burnout and we need to take time off to recuperate from it.

Next, we turn to the different ways withdrawal may manifest itself. It may be that you become disengaged at work and are no longer able to do your best work. You may go in to work every day, totally disengaged, sit at your desk and not be able to accomplish much. You might still be there physically but mentally and emotionally, your heart is no longer in it. This situation usually is not tenable; either you or the organization will quickly decide that it is no longer a fit and that you should move on.

You may have to take time off from work to recover. This could be in the form of vacation, FMLA, sick days, a sabbatical if you're fortunate enough to work at an organization that offers them, quitting your job completely, or being fired. Burnout is a work-related issue and getting some distance from work is the most helpful first step in resolving it. It is possible for burnout to be resolved without taking time away from work, but it takes much longer to do this as well as discipline in your everyday actions. Even in a best case scenario, burnout can take twice as long to recover from as the initial symptoms last, so the sooner you start to work on getting control of your life, the quicker your recovery will be.[118]

Ultimately, you may choose to leave the HR profession entirely. This could be for a period of time and you may feel called back to the profession. Or it may be a permanent exit from the field. Sometimes you end up in a different role, either in your same organization or in a totally different one. It is common for those in finance who experience burnout to quit and pursue less intense careers.[119] I have heard many anecdotes of HR professionals moving into different roles because of the pressures. Some of us pursue consulting, academia, administrative roles, other management roles, or something altogether different.

It is rather unfortunate, because there are many talented people who work in HR. The epidemic of burnout causing angst and a potential mass exodus from the profession would result in organizations not having the valuable insight of the talented people who have spent years honing their craft (people management) to help guide and direct their organizations in this challenging time with one of the most important functions of the business. Organizations are going to need good people to help lead their people. I know I am biased, but I think HR is one of the most important functions within an organization.

I truly believe, to the very depth of my soul, that we need to lead the charge to fix our organizations, our collective outlook and mindset, and ourselves in order to overcome the challenges that we have been facing in this area (not necessarily in that order). Nothing good comes of any of us

---

118 https://www.tlnt.com/c-level-burnout-a-problem-no-one-talks-about/

119 https://www.growthbusiness.co.uk/jobs-likely-cause-burn-out-2550536/

experiencing burnout. No one is better equipped to wage a war against burnout than HR professionals. We have to start with ourselves. We cannot help anyone else if we are burned out! We have to overcome our own burnout and then assist in providing strategies to help our employees and managers overcome. We need to put training, systems, and processes in place that allow us to prevent burnout from happening in the future.

Dr. Jeanine Joy declares there are three types of burnout according to the Burnout Clinical Subtype Questionnaire-12:

- Frenetic: characterized by the investment of a large amount of time to work and is common in highly involved, ambitious and overloaded individuals. 'Involvement' is the investment of every effort required to overcome difficulties; 'ambition' is a great need to obtain important success and achievements at work; and 'overload' is risking one's own health and neglecting of one's own personal life in the pursuit of good results.
- Underchallenged: is influenced by occupation type. It appears in indifferent and bored individuals who do not find personal development in their work. 'Indifference' is lack of concern, interest and enthusiasm in work-related tasks; 'boredom' is caused by the understanding of work as a mechanical and routine experience with little variation in activities; and 'lack of development' is the absence of personal growth experiences for individuals together with their desire for taking on other jobs where they can better develop their skills.
- Worn-out: determined by the rigidity of the organizational structure of an individual's workplace and is characterized by a lack of control over results, lack of recognition for efforts and neglect of responsibilities. 'Lack of control' is the feeling of helplessness as a result of dealing with many situations that are beyond their control; 'lack of acknowledgement' is the belief that the organizations those individuals work for fail to take their efforts

and dedication into account; and 'neglect' refers to individuals' disregard as a response to any difficulty.[120]

Part two focuses on solutions, which I have organized according to these three types. I pose time management solutions to help the frenetic type of burnout, career management solutions for the underchallenged, and stress management solutions for the worn-out variety. I have also included a chapter on global solutions that discusses organization-wide efforts.

120 https://www.quora.com/As-an-employer-how-do-I-deal-with-employee-burnout/answer/Jeanine-Joy

# Part Two:

# Solutions

 

# Time Management

*We're going till the world stops turning, while we burn it to the ground tonight.*

Nickelback

In every case of burnout, there is an element of time management challenges. Even if you are not currently experiencing burnout, you can still improve your time management skills. We are busy. We are all so busy. There are certain phrases that we hear and we know what it means: "I have a board meeting today," "The auditors finally arrived," "I am conducting an investigation," or "OSHA showed up today!" It is easy for an overachiever to take on more and more until their plates are too full to continue functioning. Recently, I think we have gradually been asked to take on too much with diminishing resources to accomplish our goals. That being said, Alexandra Michele points out:

> It's a common misconception that the culprit behind burnout is simply working too long or too hard — research indicates that other factors, both individual and organizational, can be just as detrimental. For example, a comprehensive report on psychosocial stress in the workplace published by the World Health Organization identified consistent evidence that "high job demands, low control, and effort–reward imbalance are risk factors for mental and physical health problems." Ultimately, burnout results when the balance of deadlines, demands, working

> hours, and other stressors outstrips rewards, recognition, and relaxation.[121]

The point is that having an overload of work is unlikely to be the sole contributor to burnout. A colleague, Kate, adds this, "People who say they are busy all the time are likely not good at time management." She goes on to quote Steve Browne, "'I don't believe that people are too busy to do something.' I have a lot on my plate, but I am mindful of how long it takes tasks to be completed, how many meetings I accept, and how to keep myself organized. Therefore, I rarely feel overworked and still accomplish all that's needed at work." We all prioritize what is truly important and make time for that. The techniques listed in this chapter are the appropriate first steps to taking control of your life, and even if you are not suffering from burnout, can still be useful time management techniques.

When you find yourself feeling burned out, one of the first steps is to stop doing what you are doing. It can be difficult when you are experiencing burnout to put everything down. This was an eye-opening part of my own experience when I moved to Minnesota. Having the time to relax and choose what I focused on next rather than having every moment of every day filled was a welcome relief. I admit, not having something to do makes me very uncomfortable still. I feel that I have to be productive every second of every day in order to be valuable. This is such an important first step and it may take much longer than you would like. Be careful, as once you cast aside all of your tasks, you may find you enjoy not being overly busy!

You will also have to step back and evaluate what can immediately come off of your plate. This is helpful for any of us to do regardless of if we feel burned out, because many of us are overcommitted compared to what we can comfortably achieve. Stop what you are doing right now, put this book down, and write a list of everything that you have to do at the smallest individual task level you can muster. It may help to categorize them based on work, home, and any additional organizations you are active in. Then go

---

121 https://www.psychologicalscience.org/observer/burnout-and-the-brain

through the list and see what activities can be delegated, eliminated, or postponed. You need to get your to-do list down to a manageable amount. At first, you may not feel anything can be crossed off the list. In that case, you may need to be ruthless about it. Keep looking for areas where you can lighten your load.

What if you started by eliminating one item from your to-do list?[122] Take one item off your list each week. Keep going until your list is at a manageable amount. It is ok to have free time at the end of the day. Remember that eliminating unimportant items from your to-do list is going to free up more time for the big important items. Going forward, commit to less. It is ok to tell someone asking you for something, "No," or "I will have to think about it," or "I will have to look at my schedule." You will not be able to commit to everything that you could do. Unfortunately, the reward for being good at work (whether paid or voluntary) is that you will get asked to do more work! You will get to choose what you are taking on going forward once this activity is complete.

Once you have removed what you can from your list, create a system for prioritizing what is left. What needs to get done right away? What is important that you should get to as soon as you are able to but does not require immediate attention? What can wait until tomorrow? Continue looking for those tasks that are not important that can be eliminated or delegated. If you postpone a task long enough, you can probably eliminate it. Harvard Business Review's article *When Life Gets Busy, Focus on a Few Key Habits*, recommends considering four different areas of your life to prioritize: personal reflection, professional reflection, building and maintaining relationships, and physical and mental health.[123] Using these suggested areas can help you to categorize the tasks you do and to see if anything is taking up more than its fair share. Perhaps take a look at different task management tools that are available to keep you on task.

---

122 https://www.psychologytoday.com/us/blog/the-gen-y-guide/201705/when-youre-tapped-age-30

123 https://hbr.org/2019/05/when-life-gets-busy-focus-on-a-few-key-habits

While it is ok to sometimes push yourself, you also need to consciously recognize when you are doing it. You will need to give yourself a break once you accomplish the goal at hand. An example of this is the open enrollment period. We all know that we are going to be exceptionally busy during open enrollment. If you cannot distinguish that time of the year from the rest of the year, you need to recalibrate what you can truly get done. If your entire life has become one push after another, you are no longer conducting a sprint. You need to repace yourself for the marathon now. Perhaps your manager or organization has become accustomed to what you can get done. It is acceptable to go back to your manager and say, "I have A, B, and C to get done. I can do A and B, but then I cannot do C. Which do you prefer that I get done?"

Kate provides another great example here. She works with clients on launching annual engagement surveys. For a lot of them, this is a huge project. They sometimes ask for her opinion on when is the best time of year to launch. She always tells them that HR usually thinks of themselves last, but here HR should prioritize themselves first. They will likely manage the project, so look at all of the priorities during the year. She recommends they do not launch this during performance review season or open enrollment or while launching an LMS integration. Many of them reach out to her and thank her as they realize they would have signed themselves up for chaos if they had gone ahead with the CEO's suggestion!

You will also need to learn to take breaks regularly. Many of us in HR do not take breaks and when we do, we cannot take advantage of break areas. If I end up in the breakroom, someone is going to ask me a work-related question, which defeats the purpose of attempting to take a break. Alan Kohll writes, "According to the CDC, taking even a five minute break can have several mental and physical health benefits."[124] Alan recommends taking a short walk, which has the added benefit of getting you away from work. If a walk is not your style, get up from your desk and go get coffee or chat with a friendly co-worker about a non-work related subject for a few minutes. Or try doing a crossword puzzle or playing a game on your phone.

---

124 https://www.forbes.com/sites/alankohll/2017/07/19/7-ways-to-avoid-hr-burnout/1

Do anything to give yourself a short break. You will reap the benefits in regained focus very quickly. Obviously, taking a short break is not going to cure your burnout. There are tactics that you are going to have to use immediately to get some traction, but overall you are going to have to change your entire way of life in order to resolve burnout and prevent future occurrences.

It will also help to draw better boundaries at work. Many of us work in salaried roles that are capable of occupying every waking second if we allow. HR is an important function and a large part of the business. We in HR are people who want to help people and who want to make it better. When someone walks through our door with a problem, we want to fix it. We see lack of dedication to our jobs at 110% as being a failure. What we do not always recognize is 100% is more than enough. In fact, 100% is even too much. We do not expect 100% efficiency out of machines or our people. Why do we expect it out of ourselves? It is acceptable to take a break. It is acceptable to walk away from your desk when you need to. It is acceptable to take a lunch that is not eaten at your desk. It is acceptable to leave the office at 5 PM. Dawn Burke shares that CEOs (or others we report to) are often sending emails at all hours of the day and night and that makes us feel obligated to respond to them and also poses that maybe it is because our CEOs are facing their own burnout.[125]

We can help some CEOs. We can coach them and provide suggestions on how to deal with their own burnout and how to help the organization avoid burnout. In other cases, some CEOs will not be responsive to help; all we can do is protect ourselves, our teams, and our organizations to the best of our abilities. Ideally, in a situation where you cannot help the CEO (or whomever you report to), you will likely begin looking for another job, because if you start to succumb to burnout, your manager is not going to help you. In this situation, create boundaries and when your manager sends an email late at night, do not rush to respond to it right away. Prioritize what is important and that means taking time away from work, whether it is for the night or for a vacation. It is also important to go into a

---

125 https://fistfuloftalent.com/2018/11/4-indicators-ceo-interested-in-burnout.html

position with boundaries to begin with. When you show the organization and your manager that you are willing to work around the clock, you have set that as the new standard for what is expected every week. Start by enforcing boundaries early.

Take your vacation time, also. It is there for a reason and those of us in HR should know that! We were the ones who stopped letting employees roll over so much vacation because we actually want them to take it. According to a study by Oxford Economics, 54% of employees ended 2016 with unused vacation days.[126] We have a tendency to work too much and leave our vacation time untouched. Schedule some downtime for yourself right now. You do not even have to plan to go anywhere. It might be better if you did not. Would it be nice to have an extra day at home where you are not scrambling to get something done for once? With that being said, HR is also sometimes the controller of flexible work arrangements, which can be a great solution for those experiencing burnout. Experiment with creative options here!

It is important to have someone cross-trained in the areas you oversee that cannot be left undone during your vacations. This will vary from organization to organization, so carefully review what you do on a daily and weekly basis and identify people that could be cross-trained to do this work. Additionally, most of the work HR does is not so critical that it cannot be delayed for a week, in order for you to have some downtime. When you are out, do not check your work email obsessively. Truly try to disconnect. Remember that your health depends on your ability to leave work at the office. If you cannot go an entire week without checking work email, try to go for a full day without doing it. Then see if you can push that for two days. Slowly reclaim space in your head that is currently occupied by work.

If you are responsible for a portion of the HR department that handles true emergencies (think safety, investigations, payroll, etc.), then dedicate someone in your office to contact you if an emergency arises so you do not

---

126 https://www.shrm.org/hr-today/news/hr-magazine/0817/pages/infographic-the-problem-with-burnout.aspx

have to monitor your email constantly. Pick someone who is discerning and trustworthy, and who will know when you are truly needed. Communicate to others that if they need to reach you, this delegate will be able to get in touch with you. Then, provide this contact with clear instructions on how to reach you. Try to make it a method that you can keep separate from other forms of work communication, so it will be evident if he or she does reach you (for example, maybe a text from his or her personal cell phone number). You also have to disregard other forms of work communication in order for this to be effective. Also, empower your managers to handle the tasks that they are capable of handling while you are on vacation. If you provide the tools and education, they are much more likely to handle what they can on their own.

We in HR are often afraid to ask others for help. We think it shows weakness or that we cannot handle everything on our own. It actually takes a lot more strength to ask others for help; it differentiates us as leaders in our organizations. Be practical about what you can achieve on your own and be honest when you need help. Sometimes we are afraid to ask for help because we do not want to create additional work for someone else. This often is not as bad as we think and sometimes collaboration offers innovative solutions. If you are in an organization that expects you to get work done regardless, then you need to seriously look for another job. There are only so many hours in a day and you deserve to sleep and take breaks from your work, too. Certainly, there are tasks that are so important that they must get done, but not everything should rise to this level.

Encourage others to take time off, too.[127] Think about both your direct reports and others within the organization. We all need time away from work to recharge ourselves. In HR, we have the ability to encourage this in our organizations. We can create vacation and PTO policies that encourage others to take time off. We can guide the organization to be more understanding about work-life balance. This might feel a little self-serving because we want to work with well rested, fully functioning employees and be allowed to enjoy our vacations, too! It makes our jobs easier overall.

---

127 https://www.forbes.com/sites/alankohll/2017/07/19/7-ways-to-avoid-hr-burnout/1

Encourage others to have people in the organization cross-trained and take breaks from their roles to relax and recuperate. When they are out, try to not ask for anything from them so they can also disconnect. Partnering together will result in an overall better organization. Ask your leaders to set the example here. Remind them that how they communicate while on vacation will influence the organization's response to this.

HR is often responsible for assisting others with burnout. It puts a burden on HR professionals to help others, especially as we are suffering ourselves. You cannot help others if you are not taking care of yourself. You need to protect yourself first. The organization wants to make sure that everything that it needs will be done and often, they view you as a resource to achieve these goals. It does not do the organization any good if you are suffering from burnout and cannot accomplish critical goals. By taking care of yourself, you are protecting one of the organization's most valuable resources: you. Of course, this is a generalization; there are organizations and managers that exist that care about their people. However, there are also enough organizations that do not go to great lengths to address burnout. Therefore, we need to protect ourselves.

Perhaps to reestablish boundaries, you will need to take a week or two off and come back with a totally different, refreshed perspective. Maybe you need to take FMLA and apply for short-term disability. If you stay within your organization, make sure when you return you have a plan in place to address your burnout and that you have the resolve to stand firm in your new boundaries. It will not be easy. Maybe you need to move to a new organization and establish boundaries from there. Maybe you need to take some time off to recover before you start that new job. All of this is perfectly acceptable and it does not make you any less valuable. You can work out a plan where you are able to do this. Remember to ask for help from others when you need it.

As HR professionals, we have a responsibility to understand burnout in others and accept that burnout does not make someone a bad employee or candidate. We typically oversee the hiring in our organizations and have some influence over the process. If we interview someone for an HR position (or a different role) and he or she has taken time off due to burnout, we should understand that does not mean this person will necessarily be a bad fit for the job. We can start to help break the stigma of experiencing burnout. Remember, good employees burnout too and sometimes more frequently. Devotion to one's job can be a contributing factor!

It is easy to focus inward during times of stress. Carley Hauck writes, "[w]hen we feel stressed we protect the Me and not the We, which does not serve anyone in the long term." [128] We have to continue to monitor those around us, especially our direct reports at these times. We need to better protect our teams as well.[129] If our employees are overwhelmed and taking on too much, we need to recognize that and take steps to help them. I know of an HR colleague who has felt incredibly burned out. She shared that her manager contacted her, crying. She realized that her manager was suffering as much as she was. However, her manager had treated her poorly previously. Why had her manager not observed the effect of her behavior towards my colleague? Instead, as the manager, she should be sheltering her team and supporting them as much as possible.

We need to provide employees with resources that are needed to be effective in their jobs if they are struggling with time management. Can you hire a temp to assist with a project or transfer someone from another area temporarily? How about additional time off after a particularly big project to help them recuperate? Maybe a one-time spot bonus to thank them for a job well done? If the organization will not do it, can you afford to buy them a Fandango gift card out of your pocket? What about a little relief in the way of relaxed deadlines? This is not always the solution, but can you take on a little extra to help them get through a project? These resources are not always available in all organizations and not all are viable solutions HR has to advocate for their teams. If we do not model desired behaviors within our departments, how should the rest of the organization's departments expect to stand a chance? This also consists of making sure

---

128 https://www.15five.com/blog/workplace-mindfulness/

129 http://fistfuloftalent.com/2018/11/4-indicators-ceo-interested-in-burnout.html

that we go home at a reasonable hour and do not email our teams at all hours of the night. Schedule your emails to be sent out at a reasonable hour if you are someone who likes to work late into the night and that works for your schedule.

I am going to put a small plug in for mindfulness here. Mindfulness is a task that I continue to dedicate myself to. It also continues to gain traction in the organizational psychology and neuroscience fields. I am far from an expert and it is beyond the scope of this book to provide extensive instruction here. That being said, here are some of the basics, so you can make an informed decision if mindfulness is worth pursuing. It also provides specific information on how it helps combat burnout:

> Mindfulness is the ability to pay attention to this moment without judgment, and is cultivated from a daily meditation practice. A few deep belly breaths and we bring more oxygen to our brain, our heart rate calms down, we let go of thoughts of the past or future, and we bring our full self to the moment and our work...
>
> Start by identifying what has priority and do that item until completion. Close your email, turn off phone alerts, and identify the time span you will focus on a task, then attend to ONLY that task...
>
> This may be helpful to say to yourself several times during your day:
>
> (Breathing In) I am aware that I am juggling numerous tasks.
>
> (Breathing Out), I am aware that I can accomplish only so much in one day.[130]

Practicing mindfulness is one additional way that we can help combat our burnout. We can better manage our time by focusing on one task at a time,

---

130 https://www.15five.com/blog/workplace-mindfulness/

which will improve our efficiency and productivity. During her interview, Sandy swore by meditation. She said, "I meditate each day before coming to work. I believe that because I'm so familiar with certain personality styles in the workplace, I have a heightened awareness, intuitiveness to move to 'calm' prior to interacting with certain people. For me, it is important to maintain my personal credibility and reputation, not only in the workplace, but in the community which I support and where I am an active leader in the industry." If mindfulness has piqued your interest, there are apps, videos, and books to help you learn more.

Finally, self-care is also important. It is one of the first items we start to neglect as we experience burnout. Continue trying to eat healthy foods and stay hydrated, get plenty of sleep, take good care of your hygiene, and exercise. Stuart Taylor, CEO of Springfox, says "the process really starts with attending to their own needs, so they can participate in life more fully."[131] Taylor goes on to recommend sleep, exercise, nutrition, and meditation. Often, if something feels off, we have skipped one of our body's main needs for too long recently. You have to prioritize yourself and your health. Create a daily routine that works for you and follow it religiously. You will find that you feel much better when you are taking care of yourself.

Self-care has become extremely important to me. I have developed a workout routine that I continue to tweak that suits me. I carefully monitor what I eat and drink and I try to make better choices surrounding this each day. I make sure I get enough sleep. Taking better care of my health has made me feel much better. The investment in myself has been well worth it. I try to give myself breaks and rest (I will be honest, this is still difficult for me). I work on my self-improvement through reading and self-reflection. I take supplements that support positive mood. I am always keeping an eye on my mental health and correcting as I need to on an ongoing basis. My motorcycle is my passion and I dedicate time to that as often as possible. It is an instant mood uplift for me when I am in need. Also, I am mindful of being around positive influences. I mitigate time with

131 https://www.tlnt.com/c-level-burnout-a-problem-no-one-talks-about/

those who are negative or toxic and I seek out positive influences. I actively work to surround myself with these people. This is an ongoing effort that I continue to develop by learning more about myself and my needs.

Sometimes, self-care can be getting a glass of wine after work and enjoying a quiet evening to yourself. It can be getting together with a friend or a colleague you have not seen in a while. It can be letting go so minor issues do not eat us alive. It can be taking extra good care of ourselves over the weekend and treating ourselves to a manicure, a day at the beach, taking time to journal our thoughts, indulging in a piece of cake, or whatever simple pleasure you enjoy the most. Whatever self-care looks like for you, make sure you are taking care of yourself.

❧

# Career Management

*That old flame may not be stronger, but it's been burning longer than any spark I might have, started in your eyes.*
Alabama

HR is a very challenging and unforgiving field. It can also feel unrewarding at times. As we covered before, many of us got into HR because we like people and genuinely want to help. Sometimes helping means that we are letting go of a bad employee so that others can be more productive, successful, and happy. Sometimes it means conducting a lay-off so that the entire organization can avoid going under. Suffice it to say that HR is not easy. When we are young and choosing a career, sometimes we do not know what we are getting ourselves into until much later.

One of our biggest drawbacks is that we try to convince ourselves that there is not a problem, that we are not burned out. We are a little tired, behind, overworked, or under the weather. We are like the frog analogy. Frogs that are slowly boiled in hot water do not react; however, when placed directly into boiling water, they jump out immediately. If we went from normal to boiling instantly, we would jump out, too. Unfortunately, most of the time additional stress (the heat) gradually builds and we are not aware of it. Then, it is boiling and too late to react.[132] Much like other issues, our first step needs to be admitting there is a problem. If we do not recognize the issue, we will never take steps to resolve it.

HR is in a strange position with regards to managing burnout within our organizations. To some extent, we are at the mercy of senior management,

---

132 https://www.tlnt.com/c-level-burnout-a-problem-no-one-talks-about/

external factors, and our employees, as to what we can do about burnout organization-wide. For example, Alan Kohll writes, "[w]ithout proper leadership, HR is susceptible to burnout."[133] We do not have control of everything within the organization. However, we are in a position where we have to do something about our burnout, and as much as possible, the organization's employees' burnout as well. A Kronos study revealed that HR is pointing their fingers at senior leadership, "The C-Suite must step up their commitment, too, according to HR leaders in the study, who say lack of executive support (14 percent) and a lack of organizational vision (13 percent) are additional obstacles to improving retention in 2017."[134] We have to take responsibility for this problem and we have to make a better case to senior leadership.

I am going to share what might be an unpopular thought: is burnout being driven by HR professionals? HR Bartender shares an article outlining five programs to reduce burnout: compensation, training and development, recognition and rewards systems, work-life balance, and mentorship programs.[135] These are all typically HR programs. Kronos survey echoes this sentiment:

- Too much work and too little pay are problematic, but many issues fueling burnout are in HR's control.
- Unfair compensation (41 percent), unreasonable workload (32 percent), and too much overtime / after-hours work (32 percent) are the top three contributors to burnout, per the study.
- Still, HR leaders also identified key burnout factors falling under talent management, employee development, and leadership that should be in their control, including poor management (30 percent), employees seeing no clear connection of their role to

---

133 https://www.forbes.com/sites/alankohll/2017/07/19/7-ways-to-avoid-hr-burnout/#3991a2c83357

134 https://www.kronos.com/about-us/newsroom/employee-burnout-crisis-study-reveals-big-workplace-challenge-2017

135 https://www.hrbartender.com/2019/leadership-and-management/employee-burnout-reduce/

> corporate strategy (29 percent), and a negative workplace culture (26 percent).[136]

Do not get me wrong. I do not think most HR professionals went into HR maliciously thinking, "Yes, I am going to create programs to drive our employees to be miserable and create burnout." Also, because these may be solutions to burnout, does not mean that they are the original cause of burnout. Maybe the solution to our burnout is closer at hand than we thought. Maybe we are that solution.

Ultimately, my message is to take responsibility for our own lives, and as much as we possibly can for our own organizations. If we are not happy with where we are at, we have to be the ones to change that. Only we have the power to make that decision. I am not saying that you control everything. I am not saying that you deserve people being jerks to you, or being stuck in a dead-end job, or needing to have a paycheck and feeling like you have to make this job work. I am saying that if you do not like it, you are the only one who will be able to change it. The world is full of stories of people who have overcome unbearably difficult situations in order to achieve happiness. Robert Sutton writes in *The Asshole Survival Guide*, "The upshot is that even if your tormentors don't deserve to be let off the hook, pardoning them for their sins can free you from being haunted by them and will bolster feelings that you are the master of your own fate." Even in a situation where we get to control nothing, we always get to choose our reaction. We have more power over our problems than we have admitted.

It can be hard to accept that we are responsible and in charge of our own burnout. Think about it this way though: there is nothing better I could be telling you. If I told you it is your manager's, nasty co-worker's, spouse's, or your parents' fault, what could you do about that? Practically nothing. You have no control over what anyone else does. You can influence, manipulate, logic, demand, and beg, but it is unlikely to change someone

---

136 https://www.kronos.com/about-us/newsroom/employee-burnout-crisis-study-reveals-big-workplace-challenge-2017

else's behavior. But, luckily, it is not anyone else's fault. It is your fault. And the sooner you accept that and start doing something about it, the better your life will be. Here is Tracy Martino's story of how she recognized the role she had played in her own burnout:

> To avoid the pain I lost myself in social media. Scanning posts one day, a Johnny Depp quote caught my eye. It read, "People cry not because they're weak. It's because they have been strong for too long." My body started to shake as I realized these words echoed my existence. This was my truth. This was when I became conscious of the reality I had been creating.
>
> Once you've opened the door to consciousness and awareness, your reality is never the same. It wasn't for me. When I shifted my consciousness, I was able to look at my journey from a place of an observer and not a victim.[137]

Begin to develop an internal locus of control, whereby you place ownership on yourself.[138] One method of doing this is to be cognizant of your reactions to small items each day. Practicing on easier challenges will begin to build your muscle for when the challenge is greater. The next time you are stuck in traffic, try to control the emotional reaction you have. Keep reminding yourself that getting upset will not make it move any quicker! Another way to build this is by envisioning situations that are likely to trigger you and imagining yourself not having an emotional overreaction to them. Practice having the reaction that you wish you would have. Remember that you get to choose the reaction you have to any situation. You get to decide if it is going to make you unhappy or not. Caroline Beaton writes it is, "[n]ot fair or accurate to say burnout is all in our heads, but attitude pertains more to how we feel about work than we might think."[139]

---

137 https://goodmenproject.com/featured-content/burnout-became-my-spiritual-masterpiece-ndgt/

138 https://constantrenewal.com/stoic-practices/

139 https://www.psychologytoday.com/us/blog/the-gen-y-guide/201705/when-youre-tapped-age-30

Begin to take charge of the challenges in your life and change them to better suit you.

This might mean that you need to do some serious reflection about whether HR is the career for you. This is a difficult chapter to write. It is hard to tell someone that the career he or she had dreamed of may not be the right one. I want to believe that any of us can become whatever we put our minds to. In reality, there are people who are in HR today who have no place being in HR. There are people who are not in HR who would be great at it. There are people in HR who need a break to continue. Some of us wound up in roles that are not a good fit for us. Maybe we specialized when we should have generalized. Maybe you are doing benefits and you would be better in employee relations. Maybe you do recruiting but your true passion is Organizational Development. Maybe you feel trapped, unable to perform to your full potential because of the organization you are with. Who am I to tell you what you should be doing with your career? All I can do is give you an opportunity to think about that possibility. You cannot go back and change what you have done; all you can do now is move forward the best that you are able to, knowing what you know now.

Choosing the next step of your career is deeply personal and obviously no one can make better decisions for you than you in this area. You have to make this choice. You have to do what is right for you. The choice is yours and yours alone. Some of you may have families to support or others that depend on you but your career decisions are ultimately up to you, and you deserve to make the right decision for yourself. You have to have the freedom to do what is right for you. Life is too short and too precious to not do it.

Do some reflection. Think about where your passions lie. Think about what type of organization you would do best in. Think about your industry. Think about your level (I will be honest, you are probably not going to be able to transition from HR Assistant to CHRO overnight; this takes time, dedication, and frankly, some amount of fortune). Think about your day-to-day responsibilities and what type of position would suit you best. Consider if you can engineer your current job to better meet your needs. If your manager is reasonable, discuss with him or her, also. Think about if this position is going to be in HR at all. We are tasked with career development within our organizations. It is time that we take control of our own career development. Unfortunately, we cannot all work for the best organizations of the world. If we position ourselves well, I would like to think that we all have the potential to influence our organizations in a positive direction. You may have to research what education and certifications you need for the career you are interested in pursuing.

Each of us needs a troop of supporters who believe in us and are available for objective advice, encouragement, and occasional gripe sessions. Find your tribe. Build your HR community. These can be family, friends, trusted colleagues, HR professionals you network with, a therapist, and sometimes even complete strangers. Obviously, we all recognize that in HR it is extremely important to recognize the need for confidentiality. Even HR professionals need someone to bounce ideas off though. Seek outside counsel with someone whose opinion you respect. See what others say. Engage an executive coach (How often do you suggest coaching for a struggling colleague within your organization? Do you not deserve the same investment?) to help you make the right decision and to achieve your career goals.

Then, sit back and listen to what your trusted advisors have to say. Listen, and hold it in your mind for a few days without agreeing or disagreeing. Think about the possibilities. Journal about it if that is what works for you. Always be reflecting on ways that you can improve and better your life. Dream about what could be. Allow yourself to dream big. What is the worst that could happen if you went for it? Thinking about the worst possible outcome is a practice known as "premeditation malorum."[140] When you think about what the worst outcome possible and imagine living that out, oftentimes it is not as bad as we initially assumed. The activity can make taking that first step much less scary when you realize that you can deal with the worst possible outcome.

140 https://constantrenewal.com/stoic-practices/

Reengineer your life. We have to get better at designing our lives and making conscious moves towards careers that work for each of us. What does that look like for you? Is it more responsibility? Less? Is it a different role? A different field? Maybe you want to try your hand at consulting. Maybe your passion is volunteering and that fulfills you and you want to do more of that. How can you arrange your schedule to do that? Maybe you need to pursue more education to achieve your goals. Maybe you need to try a totally different career, for a while or permanently. Maybe you need more autonomy. Can you ask your manager to help your current job be a better fit? Can you prove yourself in other areas to begin carving out a role that is more suited to you? Can you look at other openings within your current organization that might interest you? What can you do today to help make the career path that you are on work better for you?

Develop the mindset that you are going to make it no matter what. This was key for me when I gave notice to my job in Minnesota without another job lined up. It did not work out the way I had planned, and it worked out fine. This mindset will help you as you move forward with changes in your career to act with courage when the way is not clear. How many times have you come up against something that you thought would be miserable and it did not end up that bad? I am sure it has happened to you a time or two before. Consciously work on accepting ambiguity and uncertainty. Cultivate a feeling of well-being, of knowing that no matter what you face, you will be triumphant. Learn to harness your brain and control your thoughts so that your brain does not get the best of you. Learn to control your emotions. We tend to think that our lives are of utmost importance. In reality, our lives are so small that they barely even matter, when compared with the grand scheme. Do not get me wrong, it is deeply personal to us, as it should be. The more that we can remember that our problems are small in comparison the better off we will be.

Overall, we need to do a thorough review of what is driving our burnout and carefully plan out how we will overcome it and how we will prevent it from happening again. This is such an individual exercise for each of us. Our choice of career and how well that aligns with what we should be doing is a key part of this. I like to look at burnout as an opportunity in your life, a chance for you to take a step back and reevaluate what is not working for you, and then make changes so that you are not experiencing burnout anymore. It is your body sending you subconscious messages that something is not right. It is like your check engine light flipped on, and you are the mechanic in charge of diagnosing and repairing the machine. You are allowed to take control of your life and to make it better as you see fit.

# Stress Management

*She needs to feel that fire.*
Dierks Bentley

Stress is unavoidable today. In fact, our lives would be stagnant and boring without any stress; therefore, not all stress is bad. Furthermore, even the bad stress has positive effects at times. Perhaps we need that stress to remind us that we need to do something to eliminate it. Remember, we were designed to react the way we do so that we protect ourselves. When you put your hand on a hot stove, you reflexively pull back. When you start to experience burnout, your reaction may not be as quick as touching a stove, but you are going to have a reaction to it eventually. Sometimes, it seems like we need the situation to get bad enough before we are willing to act. Perhaps, if we were more sensitive to what our bodies were trying to tell us, we could react more quickly.

Stress takes on many different forms. For the purposes of this book, we are going to focus mainly on work-related stress and only briefly touch on how your personal life will affect your stress management with regard to burnout. My research shows that we are experiencing much more stress from work than we are outside of work. For example, 15.5% of us are experiencing severe stress from work while only 1.4% of us experience severe stress outside of work. For most of us, work is our primary source of stress. How much work we take on is a component of this, which we discussed in the time management chapter.

Our stress in HR comes from other sources, too, and I think they contribute more to our burnout than our time constraints and overflowing plates. One of our main sources of stress is from our relationships at work, often with our managers but sometimes with employees. It is not uncommon that HR professionals are loved by their employees and hated by fellow managers. After all, it is our job to negotiate between these two groups. Traditional management, with its command-and-control, top-down culture, (which most organizations utilize), means that we often have to coach our managers to better support employees.

We are often tasked with helping our managers to manage better and given little authority to persuade them to do so. Think about this: consultants can often go into an organization and create change in an unbelievably short time. It is much harder for an internal HR professional to create this change. Why is that? Why are organizations willing to pay consultants top dollar to tell the organization exactly what their HR professionals would have shared? I have a colleague who told the story of a consultant who was hired to conduct training in her organization. She knew the consultant personally and when they were discussing the training, the consultant looked at her and said point blank, "You're just as qualified as I am to conduct this training. What am I doing here?" I often say that there is a value to having someone external come in, because then managers are hearing it from someone besides me. Hopefully, when I reference that information again, it will be easier to get my point across. One of our biggest challenges is getting our organizations to listen to us.

HR is entrusted with the largest responsibility in the organization, the care of its people. We are required to walk the fine line of representing the employee and employer fairly while negotiating win-win situations. A huge barrier is that HR is rarely given the authority to do their jobs successfully. This is a generalization, but many of us are familiar with being tasked with "fixing" our organization's HR functions and then when we bring our suggestions, recommendations, and plans forward (typically reasonable ones that would move the organization forward), we are met with resistance.

Also, HR is often treated with incivility and is witness to so much of it within our organizations. According to my research, incivility and stress were correlated with wanting to leave the HR profession. This is understandable. Due to the nature of our jobs, we are often the point of contact for employees' complaints about mistreatment by management or other employees. Some of these complaints are founded and some are unfounded. Regardless, emotions are contagious and we are entrusted with handling many of the negative emotions within our organizations. Robert Sutton's book, *The Asshole Survival Guide*, says, "Assholes tend to breed like rabbits because of what psychologists call similarity-attraction effects...Such 'infection' problems happen because emotions are remarkably contagious—bad moods, insults, rudeness, and sabotage spread like wildfire." Furthermore, if you look at the professions that are commonly afflicted by burnout, they are typically professions that are stewed in emotion and responsible for processing of other's emotions. For example, SHRM had a series of articles that referred to HR as the toxin handler of the organization.[141] We are the ones who are most responsible for managing the organization's emotions.

We are held to the impossibly high standard of being "HR" and never letting our professional guard down. We have to maintain our composure every second of our work day, and sometimes that extends to outside of work. We are expected to control our emotions far more than most professions. Even in organizations where showing emotion is acceptable, to broadcast our true highs and lows at work is still frowned upon. Heaven forbid you cry! Think about that. We see employees on their very worst days all the time: the day that they do not get their paycheck, we terminate them and they lose their paycheck and their benefits with us permanently, a family member passes away and they need bereavement leave, the day they are diagnosed with cancer and need FMLA, their benefits enrollment was not completed correctly and they do not have the coverage they thought they would, they do not get the promotion they were expecting...and we are not expected to show emotion, even to show our sympathy?

---

141 https://www.shrm.org/ResourcesAndTools/hr-topics/employee-relations/Pages/Are-You-a-Toxin-Handler.aspx?utm_source=Editorial%20Newsletters~NL%202019-3-6%20HR%20Daily%201100&utm_medium=email&utm_campaign=HR%20Daily

So, what is an HR professional to do?

We need to start by challenging the assumption that it is not acceptable to show emotion at work. It is necessary even to bring our whole selves to work, to be our authentic selves. Remember Magic Johnson's story about not being able to be his authentic self and the toll that took? I often say that I do not expect employees to leave their emotions at the door; employees are human and what happens to them outside work affects them at work. Why would I not extend myself the same courtesy? The emotional situations we find ourselves in warrant an emotionally appropriate response. We owe it to our employees to give that in the moment and to ourselves to allow our own emotions to process during and afterwards. This will require finesse on our parts. The rewards will be well worth the effort put in.

Allow yourself to react appropriately to the emotions of others. In HR, most emotion is deemed unacceptable. We need to accept that we do emotional work and allow ourselves to be human. We make mistakes. It is ok to cry. It is ok if others cry. A side benefit to being gentle with ourselves is it tends to lessen our tendency to ruminate.[142] Get more in touch with your emotions and know that reacting to a human situation in a human way does not make you less human, but more human. If we are going to lead others within the organization, we must first learn to understand and accept ourselves.

Another method of dealing with stress is to work on reframing your state of mind. Dr. Jeanine Joy recommends this technique: when you or someone coming to you for help is stressed, it is because of the focus on the problem. You need to shift that focus to a more general frame of mind. She says, "As long as you are focused on the negative aspects, your brain is not going to provide you with solutions. Think about when you are at a conference where you have a lot of thoughts, you are in a state of positivity, a place of positive expectations. Then you get back to your desk and you cannot remember the ideas. Our thoughts are mood congruent.

---

142 https://www.psychologytoday.com/us/blog/the-gen-y-guide/201705/when-youre-tapped-age-30

Problems feel bad; solutions feel good." She likens it to how we experience an argument with our spouse; during the argument, you think of everything bad he or she has ever done, but when you are in a good mood again, it is like he or she could do no wrong. With practice, Dr. Jeanine says that you will be able to get to a positive state of mind within five minutes (although it may take a week when you first start). It is essential that you reframe your state of mind and also learn to help employees do the same to be able to brainstorm solutions.

One of the top recommendations is getting enough sleep. Dr. Nadine Greiner recommended in a personal interview taking care of yourself and encouraging your team to do the same. She said that not getting enough sleep is the number one exacerbating factor of stress.[143] Peta Sigley, Chief Knowledge Officer of Springfox, recommends eight hours of sleep a night and daily exercise to maintain your wellbeing.[144] These seem like easy simple steps but getting to a healthy baseline will make a difference in your overall health. Your ability to work through stress before it becomes burnout will be heightened. I can say for myself that getting my daily routine of healthy habits has helped me be in a much better place mentally. Sleep is important to me and I guard my necessary allotment in order to function as my best self. I do everything in my power to ensure a good night's rest, and if I do not get good sleep one night for whatever reason, I prioritize it the very next day. I know that I do my best work when I am well rested.

Kelly McGonigal has some interesting advice on handling stress. Kelly indicates that stress will kill you, but only if you believe that stress is harmful for your health. Not believing that stress is harmful is the healthiest step that you can take for yourself; it is even better than completely eliminating stress from your life.[145] Kelly's video is worth watching; she provides some great ideas about how to protect yourself from stress. For example, she recommends learning to view your body's

---

143 Personal interview with Dr. Nadine Greiner, November 19, 2018.

144 Personal interview with Peta Sigley, November 21, 2018.

145 https://www.youtube.com/watch?v=RcGyVTAoXEU&feature=youtu.be

stress response as positive and adaptive, and not as a negative. She shares how social support can help you deal with stress, by strengthening your heart when you are releasing oxytocin, a stress hormone that also makes us more social. She also shows that caring for others helps us beat stress. Learning to control your stress response may be one of the most important steps you take.

We have to build better relationships with our managers. We have been advising on improved ways to manage employees for decades and in many organizations, HR is further along than managers in a leadership capacity! HR's goal is to help them be better managers while staying compliant. We mean well. But where has this gotten us? All that seems to exist is a higher wall between HR and managers. Tim Sackett's article addresses manager shaming and that HR needs to stop as it is not conducive to fixing the problem.[146] HR needs to break down this wall and provide the support managers need to improve their skill sets. We need to go sit down with them, elbow-to-elbow, and help them with their business problems in order to show our value. We have to be the ones who take the first step, too.

Believe me when I say I know you may feel that you have been trying your hardest. You have dumped your heart and soul into helping managers to the very best of your ability. You have put your best effort in. This is as far as you have been able to take it with little cooperation from them. Now I am asking you to double-down and try harder? It is simple. If you do not have that in you at this point, HR is not the career for you. It is an almost impossible request in some organizations. There are managers out there who are absolutely awful. HR is not for the faint of heart though. You are going to have days when you would rather give up. No one will judge you if you do. In fact, you do not even have to publicly announce it. You can leave the profession and say you got offered a great job elsewhere. You started an HR career thinking it would be a good choice and you were going to help people. It requires more than helping employees, you have to help your managers, too. In fact, your managers need your help more, and this is the

146 https://timsackett.com/2019/03/22/are-you-manager-shaming-workhuman/

best opportunity for you to help your employees. If you do not have that in you (and picture helping your worst manager ever now), then you should stop doing HR. Period. It is tough love, but the only way is to present the cold hard truth.

Christine Porath's advice here is invaluable. Even when you are dealing with a difficult person, maintaining your composure and responding positively is a reflection on you. Porath recommends practicing radical candor. "Care personally but challenge directly." She says that the solution is to always use respect. Little steps like saying thanks, giving credit where credit is due, listening, asking questions, acknowledging others, and smiling. Porath claims that civility lifts people. "What I know from my research is that when we have more civil environments, we're more productive, creative, helpful, happy, and healthy," she says.[147] In Porath's eyes, the solution is that we all need to treat each other with more respect. This is how we build cultures that are resistant to burnout, step-by-step.

We have to get our managers' ears in order to impact change. Maybe you can do that within your organization. Maybe you can do some self-reflecting and change your approach. You can spend more time amongst your employees and better understand their needs. You can spend more time one-on-one with your managers, getting to know their perspective and how you can better partner with them. Try to find the middle ground; try to see from their perspective. We have to earn their trust in order to improve the entire organization and, selfishly, for ourselves too. On the other hand, maybe it will work better for you to look for a new job in a different organization where you can reinvent yourself and approach the challenges with a fresh outlook. That is an acceptable way to tackle the problem as well. The only unacceptable path is keep trying to do what you know already has not been working.

We do this work slowly, conversation by conversation, person by person, moment by moment. If we all put in the hard work, we will begin to change the world, one person, department, and organization at a time. That might

---

147 https://www.youtube.com/watch?v=py4P8b4t3DI

be a Pollyannaish way to look at it, but it is the honest truth. How do we make the world a better place? We start by getting up and making our bed, loving our family to the best of our ability, making our organization a better one, and taking better care of ourselves and the ones who are immediately beside us.

How do we let go of being treated with incivility? How do we teach ourselves to let this roll off our backs without affecting us? Personally, I struggle a lot with my reaction at the moment. I am passionate and hot-headed. I take work personally. I think the work I do is important. It is hard to not take work personally when you care. In fact, I think that in order to experience burnout, you have to care deeply, if you do not think what you do matters, then it is not going to affect you when you do not accomplish what you set out to do. Robert Sutton's book has some valuable advice, "Why stress about an asshole doing asshole stuff?" Brilliant. Remind yourself that someone behaving poorly says more about them than it does about you. It will not work for every situation, but hopefully, you will keep that in your pocket for the next time you need it. Sometimes, the easiest response in a heated conversation is simply to walk away and allow yourself to cool off.

I have had to carefully select my response to difficult situations. I will be honest, it has taken years of honing this skill to improve. I will not tell you that I always have a good response. Every day, I practice letting go of what does not matter. "Our society does not prepare individuals well when it comes to managing stress or regulating our emotions in healthy ways," according to Dr. Jeanine Joy.[148] I try to remember that I am doing the best that I can. Overall, most of us are not as good as we would like to be at letting go. Every day I tell myself that I am not always right and I do not know the whole story. I try to see from others' perspectives. I try to be kind, accepting, and understanding. I often fail. I forgive myself and forgive others. I am doing these steps as I write this chapter. There is no point

---

148 https://www.quora.com/What-professions-do-you-feel-have-the-highest-incidences-of-burnout-and-why

where I am done pursuing these. When I get to one accomplishment, I reach for the next. I am always trying to improve.

We should also be striving to eliminate incivility from our organizations. It is essential to learn to deal with incivility. In addition, it is also essential for us to start to weed it out of our organizations, especially knowing how detrimental even one uncivil person can be. Christine Porath has good advice for doing this as well. She recommends that we interview for incivility and check references, provide training and coaching, and develop internal civility metrics. Perhaps you need to screen for these traits before offering candidates to your hiring managers. The most important factor is having the executive team on board with this.[149] We need to address this behavior consistently. Too often, we allow someone with strong technical skills or other abilities to get away with rude behavior because of his or her "strong" performance. Incivility should be considered part of performance and should never be tolerated. No one is worth paying the price of keeping a toxic worker. Honestly, if your executive team does not already get this, you are not likely to convince them. Do not waste your time trying to change someone into a good person. Look for the quickest way out. It is not your job to convince or fix the world; you have to protect yourself, too. Sometimes the best option is to vote with our feet and leave bad organizations.

Try to slow down and learn to smell the roses. Appreciate the small things. Take more breaks so when something dreadful walks into your office you are in a better state of mind to deal with it. Put your phone down, stop looking at your computer screen, and take a break away from your desk. Remember when you are tired to rest and do not give up. Taking a step back and allowing yourself to have the best presence and frame of mind is a kindness to you and those working around you.

You know those awe-inspiring moments where life forces you to take a step back and look at what is important? Sometimes these are vacations

---

149 https://www.mckinsey.com/business-functions/organization/our-insights/the-hidden-toll-of-workplace-incivility

where we see a mountain or an ocean and we are reminded how small we are. Sometimes it is an experience, such as life or death, where we realize what is important and refocus our perspective to think about what we would do if we had an infinite capacity for understanding. We need to find more of these moments in our lives every single day so we can practice a more appropriate reaction. We need to practice more mindfulness and take care of ourselves so we are not burned out every day. We can bring our best selves to work (and life) every day.

I can say that one of the lessons I learned as I wrote this book is that helping other people with burnout is one of the best ways to process my own burnout. As I was researching the book, I talked with many people who were experiencing HR burnout. I have made deep, loyal, lasting friendships with some of the people I encountered. I got the opportunity to hear their stories and share with one another. Caroline Beaton writes, "[c]ounterintuitively, one of the best ways to take care of ourselves (and prevent future burnout) is social interaction. Workplace friendships weaken the relationship between unhealthy perfectionism and job burnout. Teachers with higher perceived levels of coworker support report less stress."[150] This is particularly important when the support is coming from above you. For example, Jennifer shared during her interview that her stress level goes from a 2 to a 5 when her C-Suite is not supportive of her. Those you encounter regularly are an important factor in your stress level. Caroline also recommends carefully selecting the people that you are around. Look for people who are positive influences, who make you feel better, and spend more of your time with those people.

Another lesson that I learned is that continuing to learn is vital. This allows our brains to think more creatively, enhance productivity, and feel better by releasing dopamine.[151] It can also be a good way to relax. Lucky for us, it does not matter what we choose to learn; learning any skill generates these benefits for us. This was evident to me during a recent conversation I had where the person indicated that she had been feeling burned out after

---

150 https://www.psychologytoday.com/us/blog/the-gen-y-guide/201705/when-youre-tapped-age-30

151 https://www.scienceofpeople.com/burnout/

many years in her current role. She felt she was no longer learning anything new and realized recently that she did not like that about her role. Continuing to learn and grow in our job, or in other ways, is an easy and fun way to help prevent our burnout. What new skills have you been thinking of learning? Do you have a few minutes a day that you can dedicate to practicing?

My mentor, Nan Poppen, says that HR is busy taking care of everyone else that we do not take time to fill our own cups. We are so preoccupied with making sure that everyone else is taken care of that we are not taken care of. We have to start putting ourselves first. Then, when we have resources left over, we can lend our hands to help others, including our HR comrades. Gbenga Adebambo writes:

> Do you know the easiest way to avoid burn out and exhaustion in life? Well, I have the answer for you-stop pouring from an empty cup. Your cup is empty...but you keep pouring! I know you, you are so selfless, and you can go the extra mile for people. You are someone who gives of yourself EVERY DAY. You give and give and you enjoy it, but you're on the verge of burnout. Being in a 'selflessness mode' gives an assumption that you have already taken good care of yourself, if not, then it is not selflessness. That is self-abuse or self-foolishness, or probably self-foolhardiness. There is a thin line between being caring and being careless, don't cross it.[152]

We have to be the solution to our own burnout problem, in each of our lives and in our organizations. No one else is coming to save us. We also need to make sure that we see ourselves as the most important person in our lives.[153] We have to learn to appreciate ourselves. We have to fill our own cups first. Our CEOs, CFOs, senior management team, and managers have their own problems, including their own burnout. We are going to

---

152 https://goodmenproject.com/guy-talk/you-cant-pour-from-an-empty-cup-cmtt/

153 https://goodmenproject.com/guy-talk/you-cant-pour-from-an-empty-cup-cmtt/

have to strive to figure out our own burnout so that we can help others. The answer is in each of us.

# Global Solutions

*I am the fire!*
Halestorm

Where do we go from here? So far, I have focused on individual solutions: steps that each of us can take to protect ourselves and our spheres of influence. I want this last chapter to address ways that HR professionals can start to work towards bigger solutions for our entire organizations and beyond. It is important for each of us to have coping techniques so that if we approach burnout we can handle it individually in our lives. The statistics are clear: burnout is a problem and its significance is growing. I think that HR is equipped to aid organizations, and society in general, with this problem, more than anyone else.

I want to share varying types of coping strategies. These can range from dysfunctional to transformational as outlined below by Dr. Jeanine Joy. Ideally, HR would implement overall solutions that resolved the underlying problem rather than other forms of coping as much as possible. However, we do need to start somewhere, which can be tough when you are struggling with burnout. The first three chapters of Part Two focused on individual solutions that can provide temporary relief to the immediacy of your burnout. Keep in mind that recovery will require more than rest in order to relieve the symptoms long-term.[154] If you are experiencing burnout right now, that is where you need to focus your energy towards healing your own burnout. Start there. For the rest of us who are not

154 https://www.bamboohr.com/blog/work-life-balance-at-bamboohr/

actively burning out, I want to focus on how we can start creating thorough relief and perhaps prevention instead of healing.

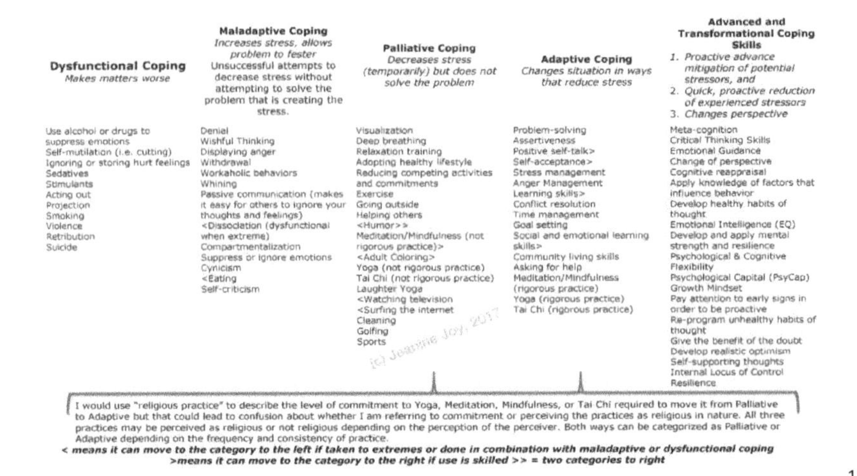


[155]

The potential for burnout is something that most of us will likely be facing for the rest of our lives. Peta Sigley, Chief Knowledge Officer of Springfox, said "We're inoculating, not eradicating burnout."[156] Her advice was to continue to invest in your own wellbeing. She said it is extremely important to recognize when you are not performing as well so that you can get to the work of rebounding more quickly. How do we move from simply eliminating existing burnout to preventing burnout altogether?

Our solutions need to be conducted at an organizational level in order for this work to have real meaning. Freudenberger thought that burnout would best be addressed at an organizational level than an individual level and proposed fewer hours, job rotating, and training as potential solutions.[157] This is some pretty advanced thinking for the 1970s! Kaschka writes, "Burnout is usually triggered by conflicts at work. For this reason, health promotion measures in the workplace have a meaningful role in

---

155 *Mental Wellness Made Easy,* Dr. Jeanine Joy, 2018

156 Personal interview with Peta Sigley, November 21, 2018.

157 https://journals.sagepub.com/doi/full/10.1177/2158244017697154

prevention."[158] He goes on to pose health promotion in the workplace, creating time models, and supervisory training. He indicates, "This brings into the picture a social component of burnout, which requires a rethink that will lead to changes in the world of work in terms of all-round humanization."[159] We are going to have to approach burnout from an organizational problem standpoint, rather than a personal problem, if we are going to have any significant reprieve from burnout.

We can conduct burnout prevention techniques within the overall organization. This is easier to do with the support of senior leadership but it is still possible to do some without it. Ideas that can be done with support: train employees to recognize, prevent, and overcome burnout, assess the organization for burnout factors and act on the assessment, coach our managers to recognize burnout in others and support those experiencing it, encourage the organization to extend autonomy to employees, and develop policies, procedures, and benefits that support employees taking time off and work life balance and decrease burnout.

Training is mentioned again and again as a method for lowering burnout rates in our organizations. In order for HR to train on the topic, we need to first understand burnout. Now that you have read this book, you are poised to better understand burnout. Dr. Jeanine Joy recommends "providing training in stress management and emotion regulation skills. Until employers begin incorporating evidence-based knowledge about autonomy, locus of control, authenticity, motivation, and positive teams and work environments into their policies, burnout will continue to lead to adverse health consequences."[160] Luckily for us, the training that we provide will benefit us personally as well. (For instance, there are studies that show that training on compassion improves the recipient's mood.)[161] It is also going to make burnout in the organization decrease and hopefully,

---

158 https://www.ncbi.nlm.nih.gov/pmc/articles/PMC3230825/

159 https://www.ncbi.nlm.nih.gov/pmc/articles/PMC3230825/

160 https://www.quora.com/What-professions-do-you-feel-have-the-highest-incidences-of-burnout-and-why

161 http://thepositivitycompany.com/tired-and-heading-to-burnout-neuroscience-offers-some-help/

in time, we will be working in a more comfortable environment with fewer stressed employees.

HR needs to take a closer look at their organizations. Find out what is contributing to burnout and begin to eliminate the causes. HR can also set their organizations up for less burnout in the future. What causes burnout where you work? You probably have some ideas already. Start talking to employees, to managers, to our senior leaders, to better understand what is driving their frustration and guide the organization to focus on alleviation. If you struggle to come up with solutions, network with other HR professionals. We are all facing similar issues and someone else has likely had that problem and found a solution. Do not hesitate to reach out to your network for help! I have never once reached out for assistance and regretted it. Even if they are unable to provide help, I leave with a better understanding of the situation and sympathy. Lastly, have the courage to start impacting change that will result in reducing the likelihood of burnout in your organization. I do not think that you have control over everything, but I do think that we are as likely to be able to solve this problem in HR as anyone will be able to.

When you see an employee struggling with burnout, try to help them. Go to their manager and assist in understanding the employee's experience. Guide them with ways to help overcome their burnout more effectively. Dr. Nadine Greiner recommends trying to see from others' perspectives as much as possible. She goes on to say that HR professionals are bad at this because, "We're busy, we're the enforcers, and it is human nature." [162] I loved that in Ingrid's story when she saw others going through what she had experienced, she recognized it and lent a hand to those employees. This can be a valuable perk that your organization offers to help boost retention. My colleague, Rachell, shares how she did that in her company, "I have a unique opportunity to make things better for the staff. It is about finding the things that you are passionate about. It has felt more meaningful because I've started taking ownership." Rachell started a program where she did quarterly check-ins with her employees. She used

162 Personal interview with Dr. Nadine Greiner, November 19, 2018.

that time to let the employee guide the conversation and empower employees. You can find space within your organization to create your own impact, replicating her experience. Finally, help to shield your own team from burnout. You can do this by seeing the signs and guiding them with your expertise. When you see someone struggling, do your bst to remove burdens from them. Take control to the extent possible within your organization.

The organization can also work to create autonomy amongst employees. My research showed that when autonomy increased, incivility and stress both decreased. Peta recommends encouraging your leaders to practice compassionate leadership.[163] Build a trusting culture thereby making it easier for others to bring forward mental health issues. [164] There is still so much stigma surrounding mental health crises that many of us are afraid of stepping forward and saying we have an issue in this area. Creating a culture where employees are comfortable speaking up is a start. Another part of this is creating an organization where people can truly relax when they are away from work. Helping to create a culture where it is expected to be honest and vulnerable is quite possibly one of the biggest determining factors in whether an employee will be able to successfully overcome burnout and stay in that organization. Sharing this and making the case in terms of ROI on retention is a good place to start with senior leaders. The next step is to increase employees' autonomy.

Finally, we need to develop policies, procedures, benefits, and other HR programs that are conducive to less burnout. These are mostly items that HR ultimately controls. HR needs to take the first step towards decreasing burnout for their organizations by inspiring change, one step at a time. Dr. Jeanine Joy recommends creating employment programs that HR professionals have control over that do not exacerbate stress. It needs to be more than providing an EAP, she said. It requires an active effort towards eliminating stress within positions and across the organization.[165]

---

163 Personal interview with Peta Sigley, November 21, 2018.

164 https://www.tlnt.com/c-level-burnout-a-problem-no-one-talks-about/

165 Personal Interview with Dr. Jeanine Joy, November 29, 2018.

Draft policies that are fair and take care of employees. Create benefits packages that encourage time off and allow employees to unwind and eliminate stress.

We must at least try to persuade senior managers to care about this. Provide them the research, numbers, and cost to the organization. Make the business case as best you can. In Peta's words, we need sponsorship from the executives because this is something that has to be built from the top to the bottom.[166] This is absolutely true. A burnout prevention training program will never be successful without support from top leadership. Building on this, Dr. Nadine says we need to "[g]et the resources. We stopped asking for the resources."[167] For HR, that means asking for training, compensation, programs, time off, and whatever else you need in order to be successful in eliminating burnout. Dr. Jeanine's approach was slightly different. To get senior leaders engaged, she suggested showing turnover, calculating ROI, cost of hire, lowered productivity from stress, the cost of mistakes, and anything that will impact the organization's bottom line that can be quantified, even if only to a degree. Infographics may be an effective way to present this information to senior leaders. "Make it glaringly obvious that the company would do better if these things were properly handled," Dr. Jeanine says.[168]

What do you do if the organization does not care about burnout? Try to get the support, conduct these burnout prevention and reduction techniques informally, or walk away from these organizations in favor of opportunities where we can better assist the organization and be healthier while we do it. You may be in a situation where you cannot do that right away, but begin planning your next move and practicing self-care for your own survival in the meantime.

If you cannot get your senior team to buy-in (or perhaps they agree but are not willing to spend the money), you can still have those conversations

---

166 Personal interview with Peta Sigley, November 21, 2018.

167 Personal interview with Dr. Nadine Greiner, November 19, 2018.

168 Personal Interview with Dr. Jeanine Joy, November 29, 2018.

where you kindly recognize burnout in someone else and ask about how he or she is doing and provide support and recommendations. You can still shield your team as much as possible from burnout. Remember that this is one of the duties of your role as a leader. Dr. Jeanine suggests continuing to informally recommend solutions to employees, leading lunch and learns, and teaching the managers. She says, "[s]elf-interest is a really good motivator."[169] In other words, make employees, managers, and your senior leaders understand what is in it for them. There is also the lowered cost of training to consider. Think about what is inefficient that is contributing to stress. What areas of the organization are understaffed? Who causes stress? Can HR develop internal training programs to help? Can HR inspire managers to check on their employees to ensure they are coping properly? Cultural change does not have to cost the organization money.

If all else fails, we can walk away from organizations that do not care about burnout to show our stance on this. Believe me, I know that this is easier said than done. You may not be able to quit your job today. That is understandable! If you are not getting the support that you need, you need to come up with a plan. We cannot keep going on like this. There are HR professionals out there who are working in positions that do not make them miserable, that they enjoy even. You can find that for yourself, too. You deserve to find that for yourself. If we collectively work towards the goal of lessening our stress in the workplace, and in our society, we will be more successful. Start by understanding burnout, then work towards decreasing your own burnout, and then begin to fix our organizations. It is hard work, but it is meaningful and worthwhile, especially for those who do not have the same resources that we have available to us. We have to do this for ourselves, our employees, and the future.

---

169 Personal Interview with Dr. Jeanine Joy, November 29, 2018.

# Appendix

## HR Burnout Survey Results

How often do you experience incivility at work? (Workplace incivility is characterized by behaviors that lack regard for others in the workplace.)

220 responses

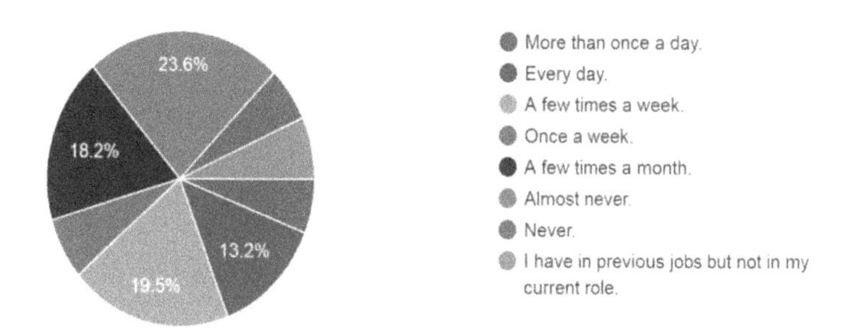


If you experience incivility at work, how severe is it?

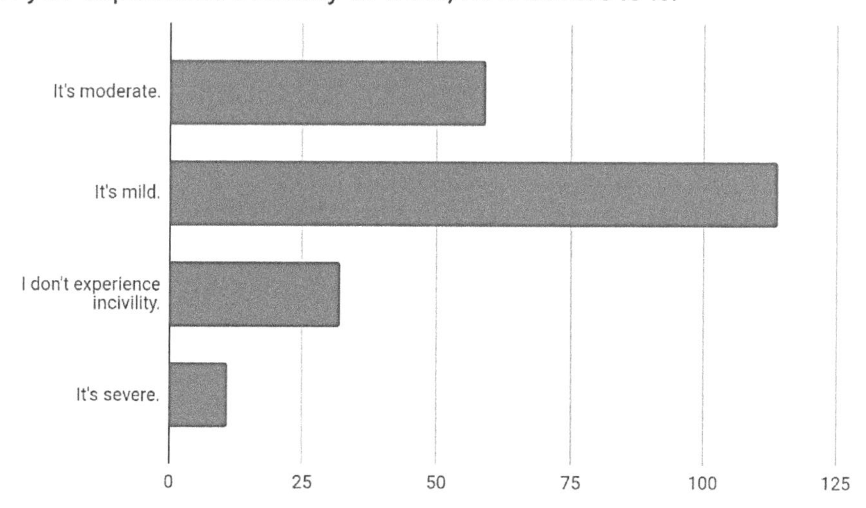

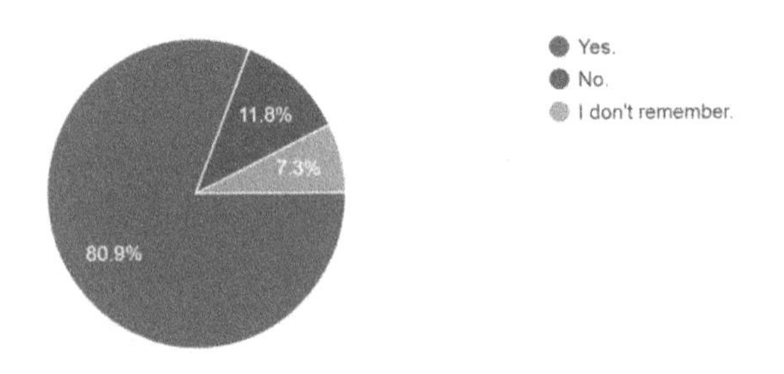
Have you ever had an experience of someone not greeting you at work?
220 responses
11.8%
7.3%
80.9%
Yes.
No.
I don't remember.

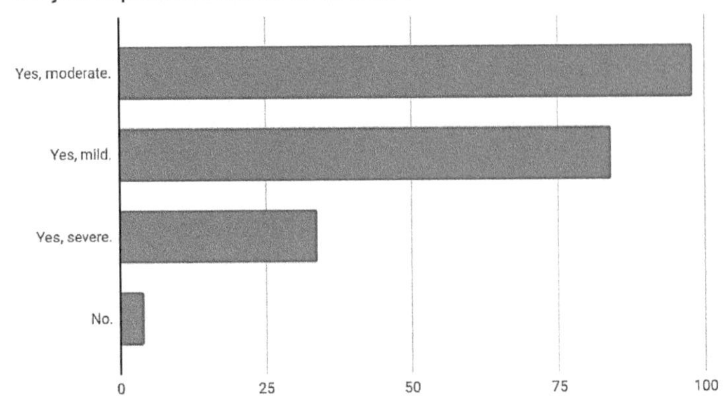
Do you experience stress from work?
Yes, moderate.
Yes, mild.
Yes, severe.
No.
0
25
50
75
100

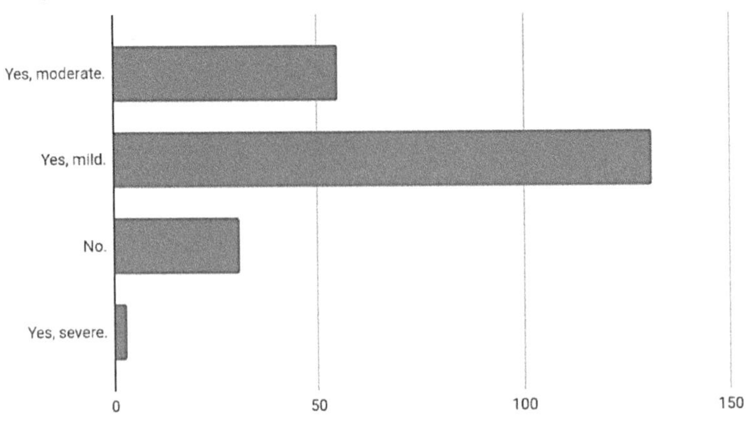
Do you experience stress outside of work?
Yes, moderate.
Yes, mild.
No.
Yes, severe.
0
50
100
150

Do you think you have experienced HR burnout?

220 responses

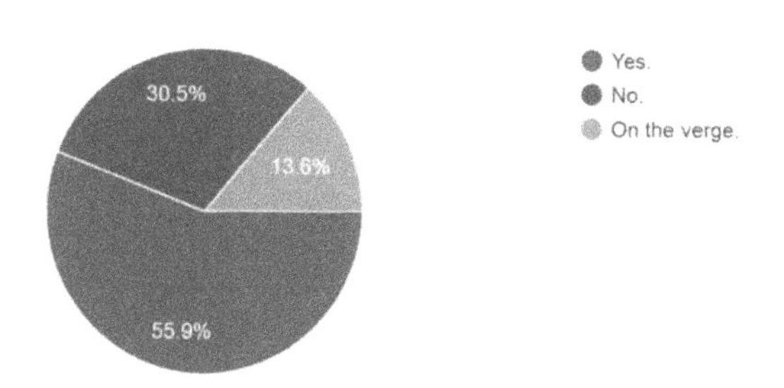


Have you considered leaving the HR profession because of HR burnout?

220 responses

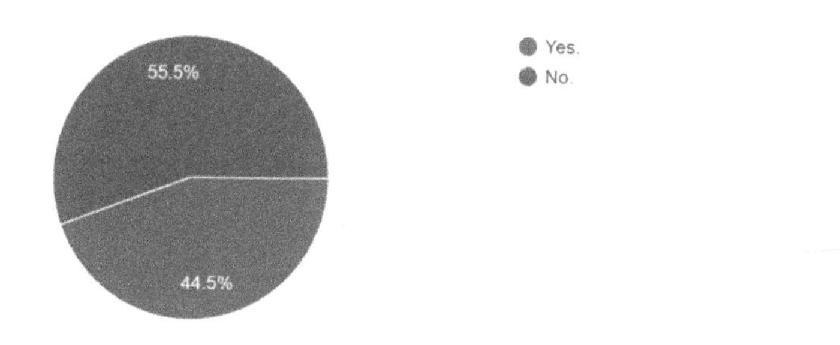


How often do you work out?

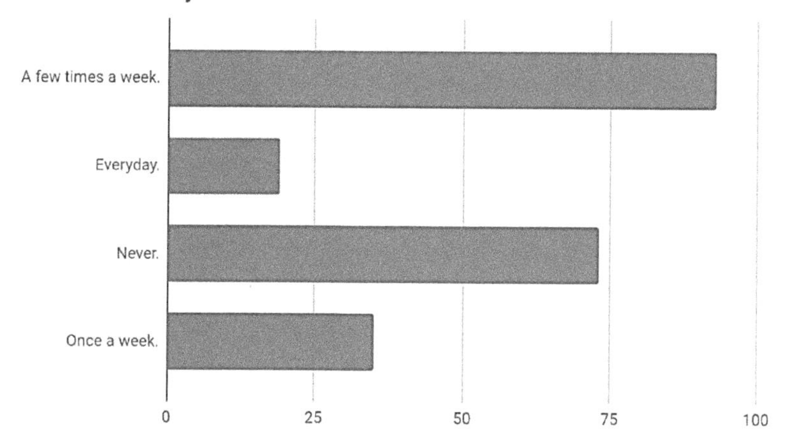

Rate your support network.

220 responses

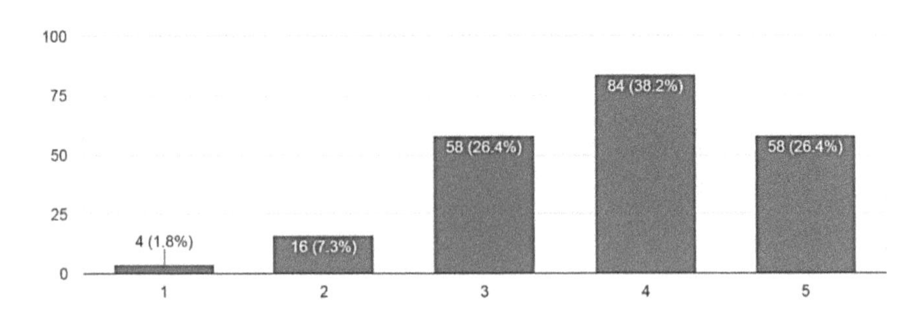


Rate your health.

220 responses

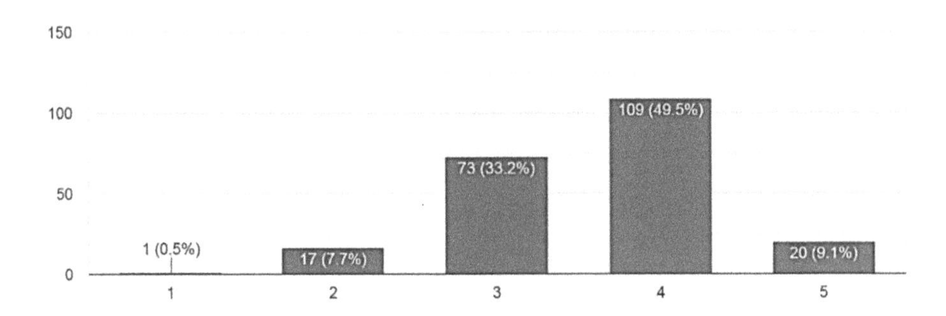


Rate your sensitivity.

220 responses

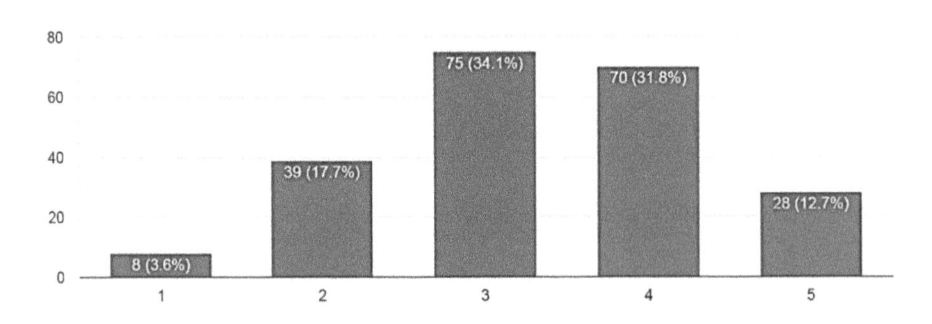

Rate your relationship with your boss.

220 responses

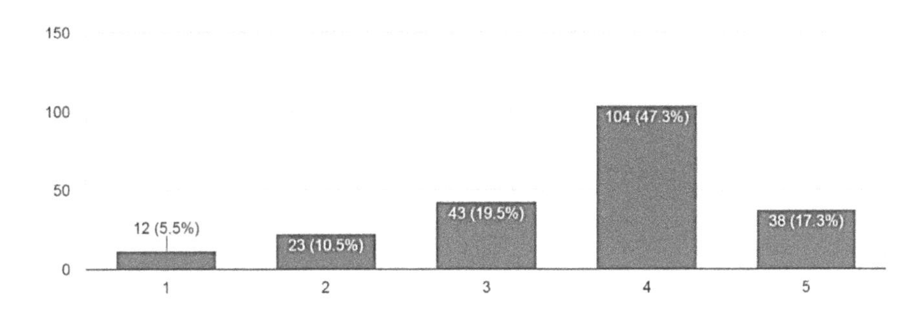


Rate your autonomy at work.

220 responses

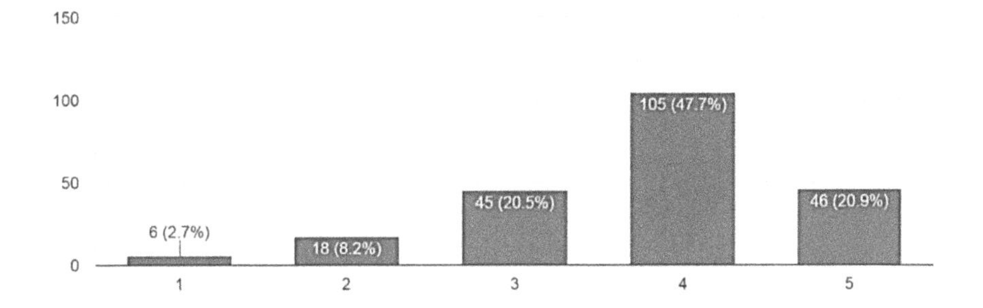


Rate your family life.

220 responses

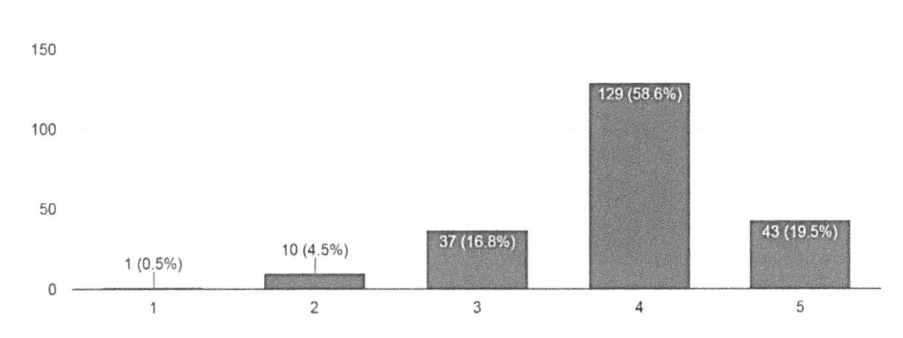

How often do you swear?

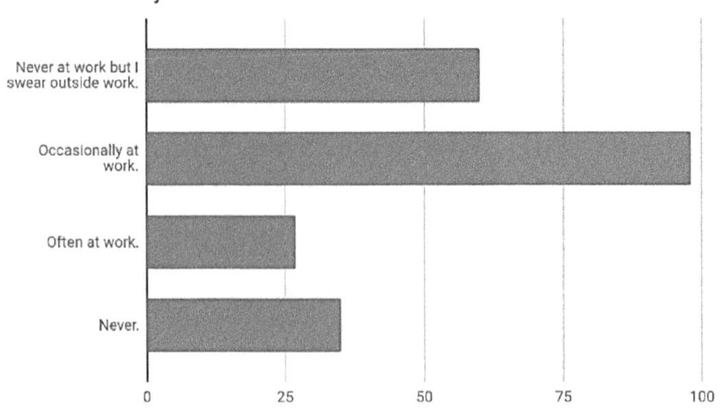


Are you financially rewarded for your work?

220 responses

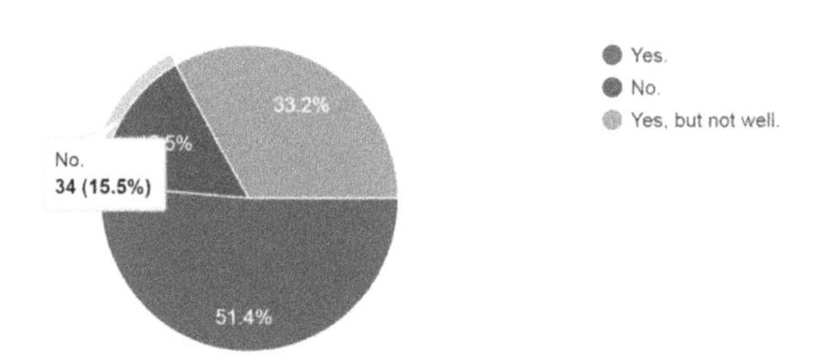


Are you emotionally rewarded for your work?

220 responses

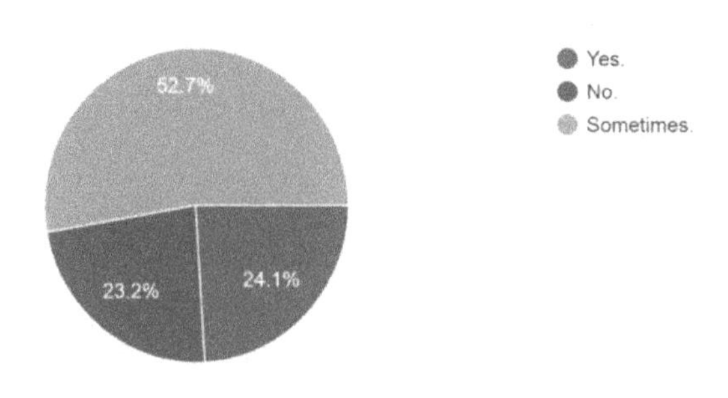

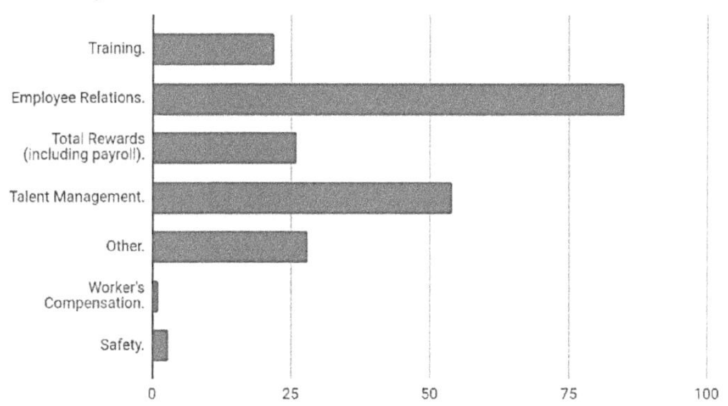


Do you feel called to be in the HR profession?

220 responses

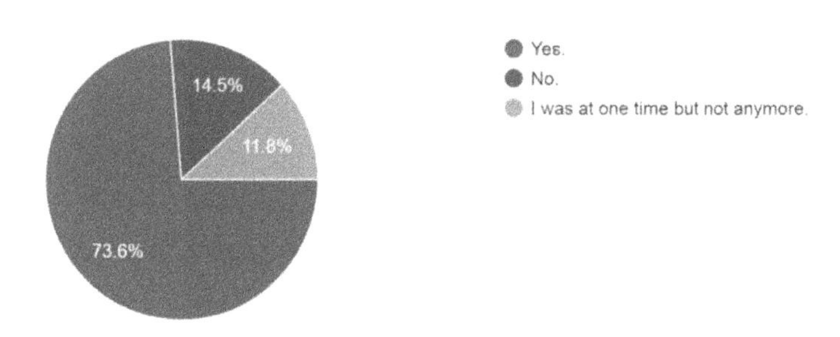


Do you have an internal or an external locus of control?

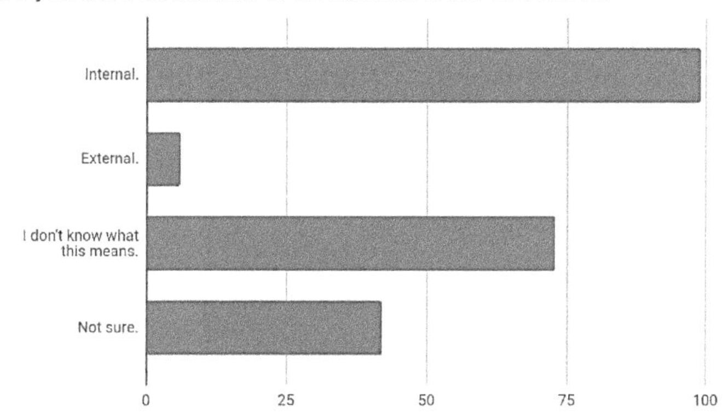

What's your job title?

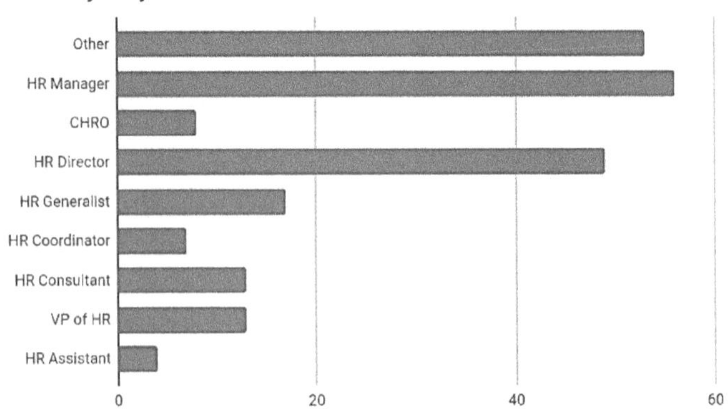


Who do you report to?

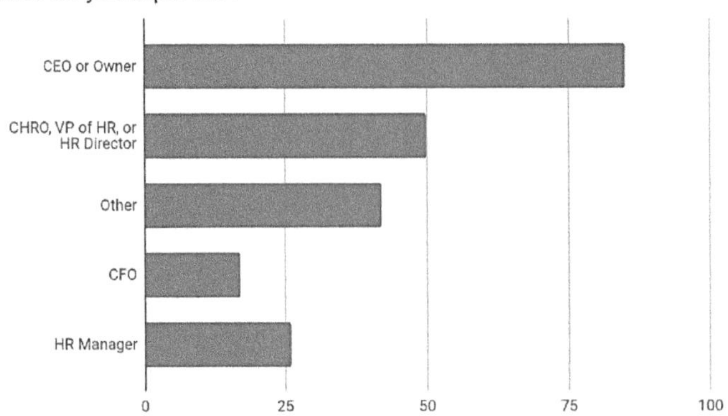


How long have you worked in HR?

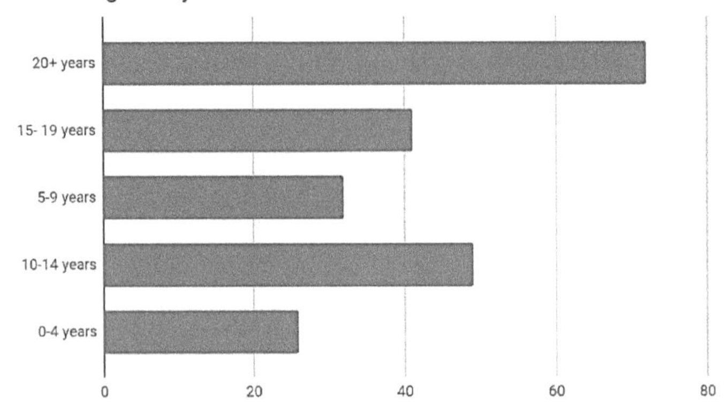

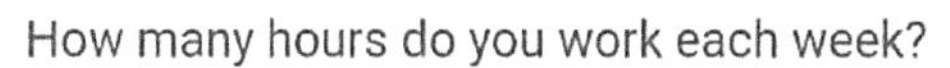

## How many hours do you work each week?

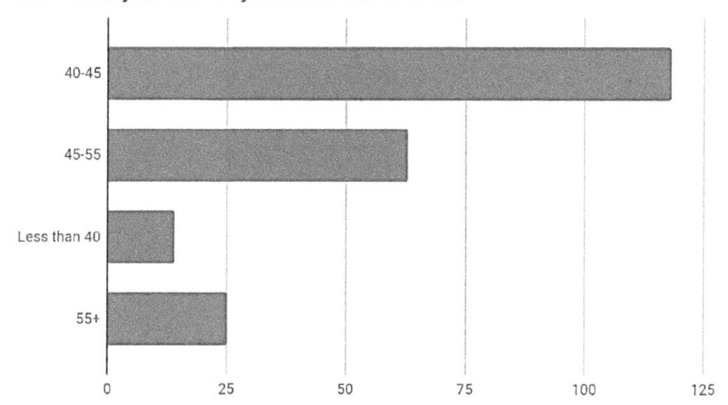


## Is your workload:

220 responses

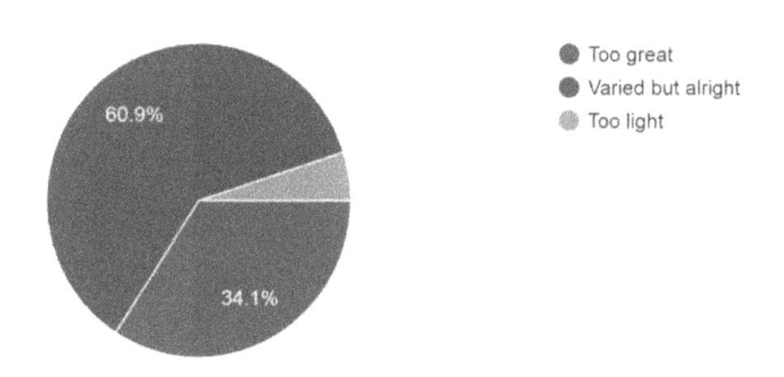


## Do you hold a degree?

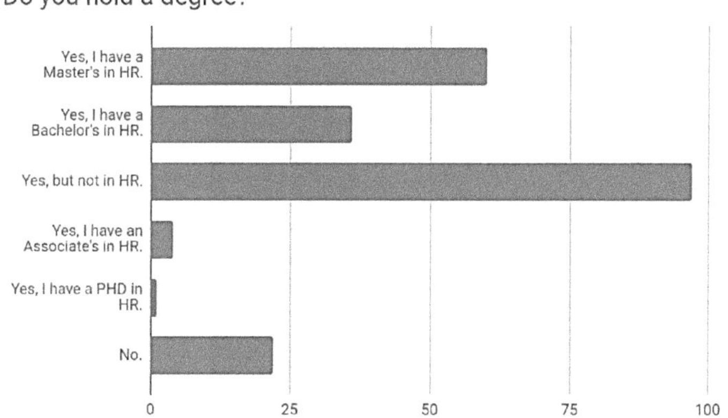

What certifications do you hold?

220 responses

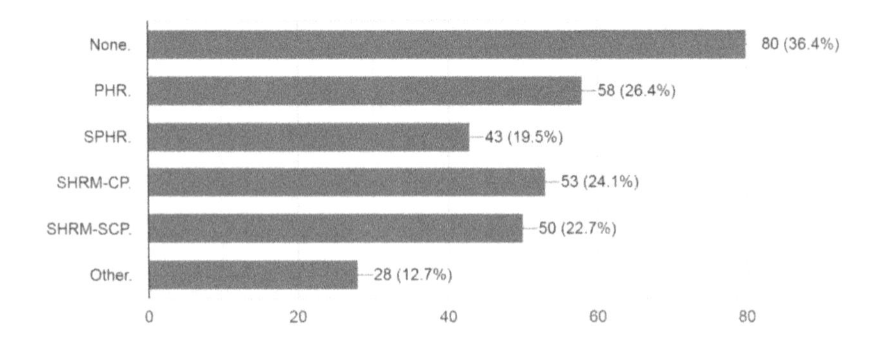


Gender:

220 responses

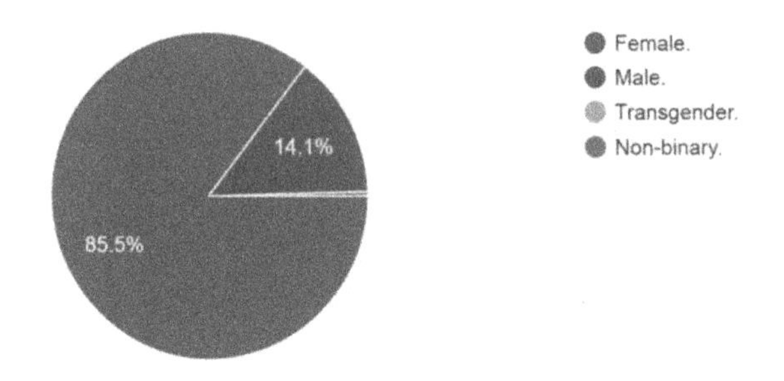

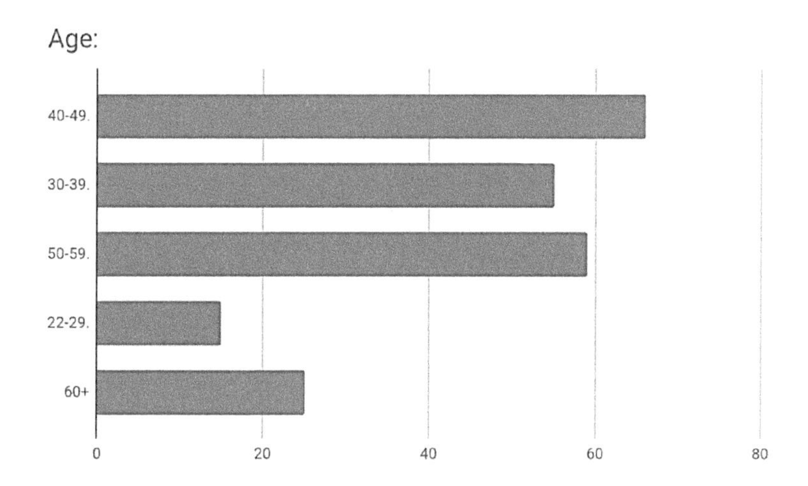
Age:
40-49.
30-39.
50-59.
22-29.
60+
0
20
40
60
80

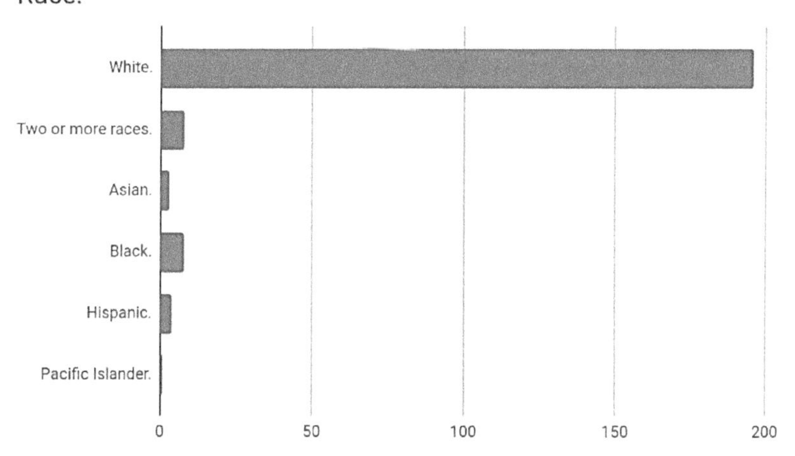
Race:
White.
Two or more races.
Asian.
Black.
Hispanic.
Pacific Islander.
0
50
100
150
200

## Maslach Burnout Inventory

(More recent versions rated from never to every day):

- I feel emotionally drained from my work.
- I feel used up at the end of the work day.
- I feel fatigued when I get up in the morning and have to face another day on the job.
- I can easily understand how my patients/clients feel about things.
- I feel I treat some patients/clients as if they were impersonal objects.
- Working with people all day is really a strain for me.
- I deal very effectively with the problems of my patients/clients.
- I feel burned out from my work.
- I feel I am positively influencing other people's lives through my work.
- I have become more callous toward people since I took this job.
- I worry that this job is hardening me emotionally.
- I feel energetic.
- I feel frustrated by my job.
- I feel I am working too hard on my job.
- I don't really care what happens to some patients/clients.
- Working with people directly puts too much stress on me.
- I can easily create a relaxed work atmosphere with my patients/clients.
- I feel exhilarated after working closely with my patients/clients.
- I have accomplished many worthwhile things in this job
- I feel like I am at the end of my rope.
- In my work, I deal with emotional problems very calmly.
- I feel patients/clients blame me for some of their problems.
- I feel similar to my patients/clients in many ways.
- I am personally involved with my patients'/clients' problems.
- I feel uncomfortable about the way I have treated some patients/clients.

Made in USA - Kendallville, IN
1167469_9780578753447
09.21.2020 0842